The AMA Handbook of Business Documents

Guidelines and Sample Documents
That Make Business Writing Easy

KEVIN WILSON
and
JENNIFER WAUSON

AMACOM

AMERICAN MANAGEMENT ASSOCIATION

New York • Atlanta • Brussels • Chicago • Mexico City • San Francisco
Shanghai • Tokyo • Toronto • Washington, D. C.

Bulk discounts available. For details visit:
www.amacombooks.org/go/specialsales
Or contact special sales:
Phone: 800-250-5308
Email: specialsls@amanet.org
View all the AMACOM titles at: www.amacombooks.org

This publication is designed to provide accurate and authoritative information in regard to the subject matter covered. It is sold with the understanding that the publisher is not engaged in rendering legal, accounting, or other professional service. If legal advice or other expert assistance is required, the services of a competent professional person should be sought.

Library of Congress Cataloging-in-Publication Data

Wilson, K. (Kevin), 1958-
   The AMA handbook of business documents : guidelines and sample documents that make business writing easy / Kevin Wilson and Jennifer Wauson.
      p. cm.
   Includes bibliographical references and index.
   ISBN 978-0-8144-1769-0 (alk. paper)
   1. Commercial correspondence--Handbooks, manuals, etc. 2. Business writing--Handbooks, manuals, etc. 3. English language--Business English--Handbooks, manuals, etc. I. Wauson, Jennifer. II. Title.
   HF5726.W675 2011
   651.7'4--dc22   2011000974

About AMA

American Management Association (www.amanet.org) is a world leader in talent development, advancing the skills of individuals to drive business success. Our mission is to support the goals of individuals and organizations through a complete range of products and services, including classroom and virtual seminars, webcasts, webinars, podcasts, conferences, corporate and government solutions, business books and research. AMA's approach to improving performance combines experiential learning—learning through doing—with opportunities for ongoing professional growth at every step of one's career journey.

Printing number
10 9 8 7 6 5 4 3 2 1

C O N T E N T S

(See page v for a list of business documents figures.)

LIST OF BUSINESS DOCUMENTS FIGURES

INTRODUCTION

The AMA Handbook of Business Documents is a desktop job aid for all corporate communicators. This book is a collection of guidelines and samples for creating a wide variety of business documents.

In addition to being the authors of the *Administrative Assistant's and Secretary's Handbook,* and *The AMA Handbook of Business Writing*, we are also the founders of a corporate communications consulting business with over 25 years' experience working for many Fortune 500 companies such as IBM, AT&T, Sony, Chevron, Hewlett-Packard, and Cox Enterprises. In our work, we've developed hundreds of business documents including Web sites, brochures, reports, presentations, marketing plans, policy manuals, software tutorials, and training materials, In *The AMA Handbook of Business Documents* we take the best of these corporate business writing guidelines and organize them in a way business writers will appreciate.

Readers can easily find information on a particular document and quickly get back to their writing project. The book includes guidelines, tips, and samples of a wide variety of business documents, including annual reports, brochures, business letters, business plans, grant proposals, mission statements, newsletters, policies, press releases, proposals, résumés, surveys, speeches, training manuals, user guides, and white papers.

We believe *The AMA Handbook of Business Documents* is an essential desk reference for the following business writers:

■ Corporate communications writers and managers

- Marketing writers and managers
- Human resource administrators and managers
- Sales representatives and managers
- Training developers and managers
- Technical writers
- Grant writers
- Public relations writers
- Administrative assistants

ACKNOWLEDGMENTS

In writing this book, we referenced many sources to confirm guidelines we used throughout our professional careers while working with a variety of Fortune 500 companies. In addition, we used our own book, the *Administrative Assistant's and Secretary's Handbook,* as a source for content on language usage, grammar, and punctuation. We therefore thank James Stroman, who coauthored the *Administrative Assistant's and Secretary's Handbook.*

The following is a list of sources we referenced while writing this book to confirm the accuracy of our content:

James Stroman, Kevin Wilson, and Jennifer Wauson, *The Administrative Assistant's and Secretary's Handbook,* 3rd ed. (New York: AMACOM Books, 2007).

Microsoft Corporation Editorial Style Board, *Microsoft Manual of Style for Technical Publications,* 3rd ed. (Redmond, WA: Microsoft Press, 2004).

David A. McMurrey, Online Technical Writing, 2009. <http://www.io.com/~hcexres/textbook/acctoc.html#introduction> See also David A. McMurrey, *Power Tools for Technical Communication* (Heinle, 2001).

University of Illinois at Urbana-Champaign. *The Center for Writing Studies,* 2009. <http://www.cws.illinois.edu/workshop/writers/>

Purdue University. *The Purdue Online Writing Lab* (OWL), 2009. <http://owl.english.purdue.edu/>

UsingEnglish.com, *English Glossary of Grammar Terms,* 2009. <http://www.usingenglish.com/glossary.html>

THE AMA HANDBOOK OF BUSINESS DOCUMENTS

ABSTRACTS

An **abstract** is a summary of a larger document, such as a report. Abstracts are also called **summaries** or **executive summaries**.

There are two types of abstracts:

- **Descriptive abstracts** are short summaries that appear on the front page of a formal report or journal article. (Figure 1.)

  - A descriptive abstract does not summarize the facts or conclusions of the report.

  - A descriptive abstract introduces the report and explains what the report covers.

    Example: This report provides recommendations for the antivirus software currently available.

- **Informative abstracts** summarize the key facts and conclusions of the report. (Figure 2.)

  - Informative abstracts are usually one- or two-page documents.

  - Informative abstracts summarize each of the sections in the report.

  - Sentence structure is normally complex and packed with information.

  - An informative abstract is intended to allow readers to determine whether they want to read the report.

  - An informative abstract is not treated as an introduction.

  - Include any statistical details in an informative abstract.

Figure 1 Descriptive Abstract

Abstract

The U.S. Air Force Research Laboratory has been developing cost effective methods for gathering occupational and training requirements information. This information has most often been collected at an individual level of analysis focusing on the more behavioral aspects of work. Recent interest in both team and cognitive requirements for work has prompted renewed interest in team task analysis and accurately representing knowledge and cognitive components of work. The U.S. and Allied Military Services have pioneered the development of exemplar methods that serve as the foundation for recent advanced training. This paper highlights recent explorations and advanced training in team task analysis and cognitive task analysis methods. Implications for increasing the accuracy and efficiency of the requirements analysis process will also be discussed.

(Courtesy of the United States Air Force)

Figure 2 Informative Abstract

Summary

The U.S. Fish and Wildlife Service published special rules to establish nonessential experimental populations of gray wolves (*Canis lupus*) in Yellowstone National Park and central Idaho. The nonessential experimental population areas include all of Wyoming, most of Idaho, and much of central and southern Montana. A close reading of the special regulations indicates that, unintentionally, the language reads as though wolf control measures apply only outside of the experimental population area. This proposed revision is intended to amend language in the special regulations so that it clearly applies within the Yellowstone nonessential experimental population area and the central Idaho nonessential experimental population area. This proposed change will not affect any of the assumptions and earlier analysis made in the environmental impact statement or other portions of the special rules.

(Courtesy of the United States Environmental Protection Agency)

ACCEPTANCE LETTER

An **acceptance letter** is often written to formally acknowledge an employment offer, the receipt of a gift, or the appointment to a public office. An acceptance letter can also be written to formally accept someone else's resignation.

Consider these tips when writing an acceptance letter (Figure 3):

- Begin the letter by thanking the person, business, or organization.
- Identify what you are accepting and explain what it means to you.
- Thank anyone who assisted you.
- State the terms as you understand them.
- If accepting an employment offer, summarize the start date, job title and description, compensation, benefits, and vacation days offered.
- Use a positive tone.
- Be gracious by showing your courtesy, tact, and charm in your writing style.
- Restate your thanks and appreciation in the closing of the letter.
- Use the spelling checker in your word processor to check for spelling errors.
- Read the letter for clarity and to check for grammatical mistakes.

Acceptance letters are typically written to accept:

- An invitation to a social event
- A job offer
- A request to serve in an honorary position
- A resignation
- An honor
- An invitation to a business appointment
- An invitation to speak
- A gift
- A proposal

Figure 3 Acceptance Letter

Evelyn Wauson
4212 West Church Street
Houston, Texas 77096
(713) 555-5555

October 20, 2014

Dear Mr. Harrison,

It was a pleasure speaking with you on the phone this afternoon.
I am very happy to accept the position of LMS supervisor with Harrison
Consultants. Thank you very much for the opportunity to join your team.
I am excited about the possibilities for this position, and I am eager to
work on the implementation of your new learning management system
and corporate online university.

As we discussed in our conversation, my starting yearly salary will
be $50,000. I understand that after being employed for 30 days, I will
receive health, dental, and life insurance benefits. After working for
Harrison Consultants for six months, I will receive one week's paid
vacation.

I am prepared to start work on December 1, 2014 as you requested.
If there is any paperwork I need to complete before I start work, or if
you need any additional information, please contact me.

I appreciate the help your associate Ken Knox provided by referring
me to you for this position.

Thank you.

Evelyn Wauson
Evelyn Wauson

ACKNOWLEDGMENT LETTER

An **acknowledgment letter** is a response that clarifies what is expected from you. An acknowledgment letter should be sent within two days of receiving the original letter, report, order, or request.

Consider these tips when writing an acknowledgment letter (Figure 4):

- Include a short apology if the acknowledgement letter is delayed.

- If you are responding to a complaint, be courteous and apologize for any inconvenience or problem.

- Be sincere.

- The letter should be addressed to a specific person if possible.

Acknowledgment letters are typically written to:

- Accept a request to serve in an honorary position or a resignation.

- Express appreciation for a suggestion.

- Acknowledge a customer's order or donation or payment of an overdue balance.

- Acknowledge the receipt of a report or letter, the receipt of a résumé, or the return of an item for refund, exchange, or credit.

- Confirm an appointment or meeting, a business agreement, or an error, revision, or correction.

- Celebrate an anniversary of employment.

Figure 4 Acknowledgment Letter

Isha Foundation
951 Isha Lane
McMinnville, TN 37110

August 20, 2014

Jeff Collins
3111 North Amber Lane
Nashville, TN 37213

Subj.: Tax Year 2014

Dear Mr. Collins,

Thank you for your recent donation of $500 for our outreach program,
Isha Care. Your gift will allow us to continue our efforts to provide free
medical care to the residents of rural Tennessee.

Your donation is fully tax-deductible, and this letter may serve as
a receipt for your tax records. This letter also verifies that you have
not received any tangible benefits in return for your donation.

Your generous gift assures a continued investment in the future of
Tennessee.

Thank you.

Dr. Jane Morgan
Dr. Jane Morgan
President, Isha Foundation Inc. USA

ADJUSTMENT LETTER

Adjustment letters are responses to written complaints. The purpose of such letters is to acknowledge the complaint. The letter is also a legal document that records what action will be taken.

Consider these tips when writing an adjustment letter (Figure 3.5):

- Reference the date of the original complaint letter.

- The letter should review the facts of the case and offer an apology for any inconvenience.

- When there is no truth to the complaint, courteously explain the reasons as clearly as possible.

- When the customer's request is denied, offer some compensation or advice.

- Take a positive approach to the letter to counter any negative feelings of the reader.

- The solution is more important than the reasons why something occurred.

- Cordially conclude the letter and express confidence that you and the reader can continue doing business.

Adjustment letters are typically written to apologize for:

- A defective or damaged product

- A missed deadline

- Making a mistake on a customer's account

- A shipping error

- Damaged property

- Poor quality or service

Figure 5 Adjustment Letter

Snack Makers, Inc.
1234 West Main Street
Los Angeles, CA 90036

April 20, 2012

Mr. Carl Luntz
Store Manager
Luntz Grocery
2411 Third Avenue
Atlanta, GA 30134

Dear Mr. Luntz:
I would like to apologize for the damaged shipment of Humus Chips.
At Snack Makers, we always try to package our product as securely
as possible, but it appears this time we failed.

We have shipped a replacement case of Humus Chips today at no charge.
You should receive them within two days. There's no need to return the
damaged product. You may dispose of the crushed chips anyway you
wish.

Being a new company with a new product, we want you to know that
we value your business and will do everything we can to make sure
this doesn't happen again.

In addition, I am crediting your account for $155 to reflect a 20% discount
off your original order.

I hope you will accept my apologies and will continue to do business with
Snack Makers.

Sincerely,

Morton Boyd

Morton Boyd
President
Snack Makers, Inc.

ANNOUNCEMENT LETTER

Announcement letters should be written in a straightforward and concise style so that readers can get information quickly.

Consider these tips when writing announcement letters (Figure 6):

- For positive announcements, make the letter inviting and to the point.
- Build morale, confidence, and goodwill.
- When announcing achievements, try to motivate others to achieve the same goals.
- Use the announcement to promote your business.
- Include enough information so that you don't have to answer questions about the announcement later.
- When announcing bad news, be considerate and respectful.

Announcement letters are typically written to announce:

- A new address
- A change in company name
- The business schedule
- A new hire or promotion
- An employee's special achievement
- A retirement
- A new product
- A new store opening
- A layoff
- A store closing
- A new policy
- A contest winner
- A price change
- Bad news to employees
- A training session

Figure 6 Announcement Letter

System Golf Supplies
4143 Green Avenue
Baltimore, MD 21205

May 22, 2012

Ms. Susan Jones
Manager
Jones Golfing
1322 North Pleasant Street
Baltimore, MD 21075

Dear Ms. Jones:

Due to increased costs for materials used in our manufacturing process, we must unfortunately increase the wholesale cost of our products. We have examined other ways to reduce our manufacturing costs; however, we have been unable to reduce costs enough without sacrificing quality. To maintain the superior quality of our products, we must raise our prices. I have enclosed a new price list that will go into effect on July 1, 2012. Any orders placed between now and July 1 will be honored at our previous prices.

We want to thank you for your business in the past, and we hope you understand the necessity for this increase.

Sincerely,

Carl Richardson

Carl Richardson
Sales Manager
System Golf Supplies

ANNUAL REPORT

An **annual report** is a document used to disclose corporation information to shareholders—a state-of-the-company report. All U.S. companies that issue publicly traded stock are required to file an annual report with the Securities and Exchange Commission (SEC). The document that is filed with the SEC is the Form 10-K.

Many nonprofit organizations, foundations, and charities produce annual reports to assess their performance. Nonprofit annual reports include the following sections (Figures 7–11):

- Letter from the chairman of the board
- A description of the charity, its causes, actions, and accomplishments for the year
- The financial statement:
    - A letter from the organization's CPA
    - Income statement
    - Balance sheet
- A list of directors and officers

If a company is privately owned but has more than 500 shareholders and over $10 million in assets, it is also required to file an annual report.

In addition to Form 10-K annual reports, the same mandated corporations must also file a quarterly Form 10-Q as a quarterly report.

The annual reports required by the SEC follow a strict format and include the following sections (Figures 7–11):

- Business overview
- Risk factors
- Unresolved staff comments
- Properties
- Legal proceedings

- Submission of matters to a vote by shareholders

- Market for the company's common equity

- Related stockholder matters

- Management's discussion and analysis of financial conditions and the results of operations

- Disclosures about market risk

- Financial statements and supplementary data

- Changes in accounting

- Controls and procedures

- Other information

- Directors, executive officers, and corporate governance

- Executive compensation

- Security ownership of stock by management and certain beneficial owners

- Relationships and related transaction and director independence

- Accounting fees and services

- Exhibits and financial statement schedules

(text continues on page 18)

Figure 7 Annual Report Cover Page

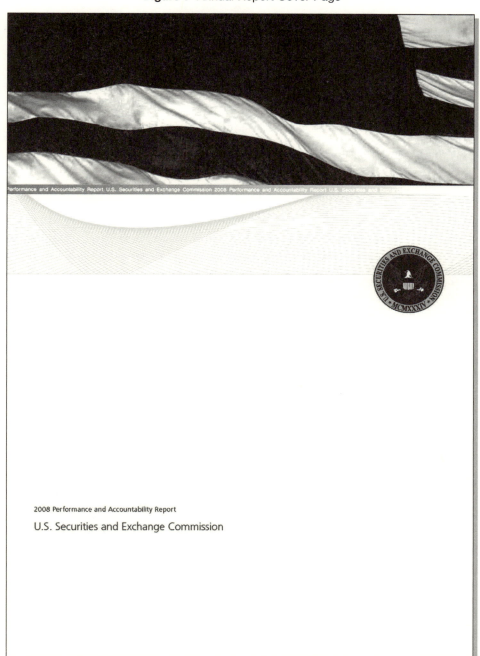

(Courtesy of the U.S. Securities and Exchange Commission)

Figure 8 Annual Report Table of Contents

CONTENTS

(Courtesy of the U.S. Securities and Exchange Commission)

Figure 9 Annual Report Letter from the Chairman

Message from the Chairman

Christopher Cox
Chairman

Dear Investor,

The mortgage meltdown and ensuing global credit crisis during the past year have confronted our markets with unprecedented challenges. The government's response to the financial turmoil has been equally unprecedented: the Federal Reserve and the Department of the Treasury have together committed over one trillion dollars in taxpayer funds to support insurance companies, banks, thrifts, investment banks, and mortgage giants Fannie Mae and Freddie Mac.

The Emergency Economic Stabilization Act (EESA), signed into law in October 2008, gives the Chairman of the SEC a formal oversight role with respect to the Troubled Asset Relief Plan administered by the Department of the Treasury. In addition, the Housing and Economic Recovery Act of 2008 gives the SEC Chairman similar oversight and advisory responsibilities with respect to the conservatorship of Fannie Mae and Freddie Mac supervised by the Federal Housing Finance Agency. These duties come in addition to the new responsibilities the SEC is already discharging as the statutory regulator of credit rating agencies, and the mandate that the EESA has given the agency to report by January 1, 2009, on the results of a congressionally-mandated study of fair value accounting.

Response to the Credit Crisis

The agency has taken a number of other actions in recent months to address significant issues that have arisen in the credit crisis. When the auction rate securities market froze early in 2008, the Enforcement Division immediately commenced investigations of potential securities law

violations by the largest sellers of these instruments. Preliminary settlements were reached in principle with six of the largest firms, which would return more than $50 billion to injured investors and make these settlements, when concluded, by far the largest in the agency's history. (While settlements in principle were reached during FY 2008, the amounts were not included in the enforcement statistics for this report because they were not finalized by the close of the fiscal year on September 30.)

As of the close of FY 2008, the Commission had over 50 pending subprime-related investigations involving lenders, investment banks, credit rating agencies, insurers, and broker-dealers. During the past year the SEC charged the managers of two Bear Stearns hedge funds in connection with last year's collapse of those funds. The Commission returned $356 million to investors harmed when Fannie Mae issued false and misleading financial statements. And the Division of Enforcement is currently in the midst of a nationwide investigation of potential fraud and manipulation of securities in some of the nation's largest financial institutions through abusive short selling and the intentional spreading of false information.

As part of this aggressive law enforcement investigation into potential manipulation during the subprime crisis, the Commission approved orders requiring hedge funds, broker-dealers and institutional investors to file statements under oath regarding trading and market activity in the securities of financial firms. The orders cover not only equities but also credit default swaps. To assist in analyzing this information, the SEC's Office of Information Technology is working with the Enforcement Division to create a common database of trading information, audit trail data, and credit default swaps clearing data. Our Office of Economic Analysis is also supporting this effort by helping to analyze the data across markets for possible manipulative patterns in both equity securities and derivatives.

During FY 2008, the Enforcement Division also brought the highest number of insider trading cases in the agency's history. In addition, the SEC brought a record-high number of enforcement actions against market manipulation in 2008, including a precedent-setting case against a Wall

(Courtesy of the U.S. Securities and Exchange Commission)

Figure 10 Annual Report Organizational Overview

Vision, Mission, Values, and Goals

Vision

The Securities and Exchange Commission (SEC) aims to be the standard against which federal agencies are measured. The SEC's vision is to strengthen the integrity and soundness of U.S. securities markets for the benefit of investors and other market participants, and to conduct its work in a manner that is as sophisticated, flexible, and dynamic as the securities markets it regulates.

Mission

The mission of the SEC is to protect investors; maintain fair, orderly, and efficient markets; and facilitate capital formation.

Values

In managing the evolving needs of a complex marketplace and in pursuing its mission, the SEC embraces the following values:

- Integrity
- Accountability
- Fairness
- Resourcefulness
- Teamwork
- Commitment to Excellence

Goals

- **Enforce compliance with federal securities laws**
  The Commission seeks to detect problems in the securities markets, prevent and deter violations of federal securities laws, and alert investors to possible wrongdoing. When violations occur, the SEC aims to take prompt action to halt the misconduct, sanction wrongdoers effectively, and, where possible, return funds to harmed investors.

- **Promote healthy capital markets through an effective and flexible regulatory environment**
  The savings and investments of every American are dependent upon healthy capital markets. The Commission seeks to sustain an effective and flexible regulatory environment that will facilitate innovation, competition, and capital formation to ensure that our economy can continue to grow and create jobs for our nation's future. Enhancing the productivity of America is a key goal that the SEC works to achieve by increasing investor confidence in the capital markets.

- **Foster informed investment decision making**
  An educated investing public ultimately provides the best defense against fraud and costly mistakes. The Commission works to promote informed investment decisions through two main approaches: reviewing disclosures of companies and mutual funds to ensure that clear, complete, and accurate information is available to investors; and implementing a variety of investor education initiatives.

- **Maximize the use of SEC resources**
  The investing public and the securities markets are best served by an efficient, well-managed, and proactive SEC. The Commission strives to improve its organizational effectiveness by making sound investments in human capital and new technologies, and by enhancing internal controls.

2008 Performance and Accountability Report

(Courtesy of the U.S. Securities and Exchange Commission)

Figure 11 Annual Report Overview of Organization's Performance

Financial and Performance Highlights

- In FY 2008, the SEC was authorized by Congress to spend $906 million, a 2.8 percent increase over the $881.6 million authorized in FY 2007. Funding was offset by fees collected by the SEC. Of the total authority, $843 million was new budgetary authority and the remaining $63 million was carried over from prior year unobligated balances, as illustrated in *Chart 1.2*.

- In FY 2008, the SEC reduced its year-end unobligated balance over previous levels through rigorous oversight and management of budgetary resources made possible by improvements in technology such as the agency's budget and performance tool.

- The SEC employed 3,511 FTE in FY 2008. This represents an increase of 46 FTE over FY 2007.

- In 2002, Congress set by law the aggregate amounts the SEC is to collect annually through fees. These target amounts generally exceed the level of funding appropriated to the SEC, and are used by Congress to offset SEC and other federal spending.

- In order to meet the offsetting collections target in FY 2008, the SEC lowered the rates of fees it collects on securities transactions on the exchanges and certain over-the-counter markets. Additional discussion of the fees collected by the SEC can be found in *Note 1.L. Accounts Receivable and Allowance for Uncollectible Accounts* on page 66, and *Note 1.S. Revenue and Other Financing Sources* on page 68.

- While the transaction fee rate was cut by more than half from this time last year, there was significantly more transactional volume compared to last year. Therefore, the total collections dropped only 36 percent. In accordance with law, the SEC collected fees in excess of its appropriations from Congress. However, the excess amount is declining, as illustrated in *Chart 1.3*.

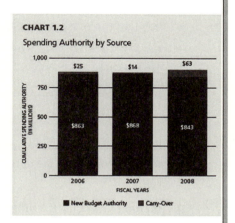

CHART 1.2

Spending Authority by Source

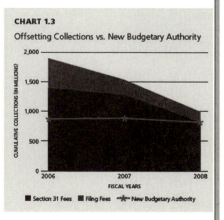

CHART 1.3

Offsetting Collections vs. New Budgetary Authority

2008 Performance and Accountability Report

(Courtesy of the U.S. Securities and Exchange Commission)

APPLICATION LETTER

In an **application letter** (Figure 12):

- In the first sentence, state what you are applying for.

- Explain the reasons you are applying and be specific.
  - Give the reasons why you are qualified including your experience, qualifications, accomplishments, and goals.

- Identify the response you would like to your letter.

- Identify the date you need a response.

- Reference any other materials included with the letter, such as a résumé, job application form, letters of recommendation, or work samples.

- Include your contact information and when you are available.

- Close the letter with a thank you.

Application letters are typically written to apply for:

- Employment

- Admission to a school

- Admission to a club

- A foreign work permit

- A grant

- A scholarship

- A travel visa

- A special program

- Credit

Figure 12 Application Letter

1322 Forest Lane
Dallas, TX 75214
August 11, 2012

Michele Phillips
APS Software
13211 Greenville Avenue
Dallas, TX 75212

Dear Ms. Phillips:

I am writing to apply for the position you advertised on Monster.com for a quality control manager. As you will see in my résumé, I have the experience to fill this position.

For the past ten years, I have been working in the information technology department at Hopewell Industries where I have been a software developer, project manager, and manager of QC Testing. My experience has ranged from coding, to managing teams of programmers, to creating test plans, running tests, and managing testers.

Recently, Hopewell Industries decided to outsource the IT function to IBM. While I am sad to leave the company, I am looking forward to a new assignment with fresh faces and new projects.

I have heard about APS Software in various trade journals and would be very interested in becoming part of your team. APS is well known for innovative quality products, and I am excited about the possibility of becoming a part of your success story.

I hope you'll give me an opportunity to discuss my qualifications and experience. I can be reached at (214) 555-5555 after 6 p.m.

Thank you very much for your consideration for this position.

Sincerely yours,

Alice Grassley
Alice Grassley

Encl.: résumé

BROCHURES

Brochures are often used by businesses to advertise products and services. There are several different types of brochures:

- Leave-behind brochures are left after a personal sales presentation.
  - These focus on a full description of the product and its benefits.
  - They echo the sales pitch given by the salesperson.
- Point-of-sale brochures are designed to catch your interest while waiting in line to check out in a store.
  - They are visually appealing with a catchy headline.
- Inquiry response brochures are sent to people who have asked for information about a product.
  - These brochures focus on a sales pitch that encourages the reader to take the next step and purchase the product or service.
- Direct mail brochures are sent to potential customers along with a sales letter.
- Sales support brochures are used by salespeople during their presentations.

In the planning phase of brochure creation, consider the following:

- Determine what you want the brochure to do: get orders, inform, get appointments.
- Determine the audience for the brochure and why they should be interested in your product or service.
- Develop an outline and divide the content you want to cover into sections.
- Consider the style of brochure you plan to create, and think about the content that is best for the cover, inside pages, and back cover.
  - Also consider content that is suitable for any sidebars.
- Determine whether photography or illustrations can be used.
  - If photography is used, also include captions for each photo that focus on benefits.
  - Photos should be at least 300 dpi resolution in order to print with the best possible print quality.

When writing copy for a brochure, keep the following in mind (see Figures 13 and 14):

- Write from the reader's point of view.

  - As the reader unfolds the brochure, present the information in the order that a reader would want to receive it.

  - On the cover or first page of the brochure, motivate readers to open the brochure and seek out additional information.

- For a brochure longer than eight or more pages, include a list of contents highlighted in bold and separated from the rest of the copy.

- Describe the product or service in terms of what it means to the potential customer.

  - Focus on the benefits rather than the features.

- Include helpful reference information that will make the reader want to keep the brochure on file.

- Write in an informal matter-of-fact style, as if you are having a one-on-one conversation with someone.

- Share your emotions and enthusiasm about the product or service.

- Don't waste time on all the details; instead, focus on the key selling points.

- Organize the content into easily identifiable sections.

- Ask for an order and provide simple instructions on how to order.

- Make a persuasive sales pitch.

In designing the brochure and doing the layout, consider the following:

- Study brochures from other companies and determine which designs are effective and which are not.

- Avoid packing in too much content.

  - Empty space is okay.

- Avoid using too many graphical boxes and lines to separate chunks of content.

  - They tend to make your design look cluttered.

- Use a consistent typeface throughout the brochure.

- You can change fonts within the same typeface family in various places for emphasis.
- Consider different fonts, font styles, sizes, and colors for key selling points and headings.
  - Use these techniques sparingly for greater emphasis.
  - Avoid all caps. Use bold style instead.
  - Avoid underlining. Use italics style instead.
  - Avoid putting text over images unless you make the image at least 80% transparent.
  - Avoid putting text columns on the first page or cover.
  - Use no more than 10 words on the cover.
  - Don't use more than two or three sentences per paragraph with a layout that is no more than nine or ten lines of type.
  - Add a space between paragraphs and do not indent the first word.
  - Use only one space after a period before starting the next sentence.
- If you have to start a sentence with a number, write it out.

Incorrect: 50% of the homeowners experienced hail damage.

Correct: Fifty percent of the homeowners experienced hail damage.

- Consider the use of multiple ink colors and colored paper.
- When creating a layout with photography, don't position the photos so that they are creased by a fold in the paper.
- Use desktop publishing software such as Microsoft Publisher, Adobe InDesign, or QuarkXPress.
  - Set the paper size before any design elements are created.
  - Confirm that the printer will be able to print on the intended size paper.
- Allow for print bleed in order to achieve edge-to-edge printing.
  - To create print bleed, expand your brochure design slightly beyond the edge of the paper with nonessential design elements to allow for trimming.
- Proofread your final design several times to avoid printing a brochure with a mistake or typo.

Figure 13 Brochure

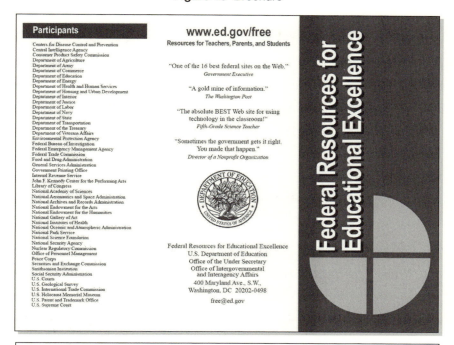

(Courtesy of the U.S. Department of Education)

Figure 14 Brochure

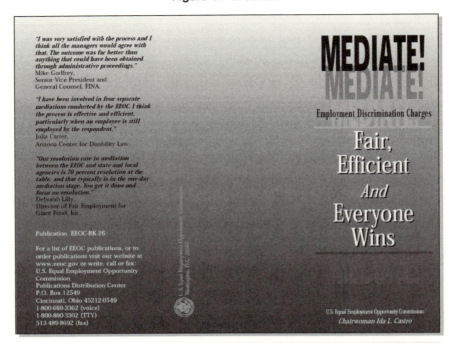

(Courtesy of the U.S. EEOC)

BUSINESS LETTER

The parts of a **business letter** are (Figure 15):

- Address or letterhead—usually a preprinted letterhead with the organization's name and address. (If letterhead is not used, include the address of the writer along with the date.)
- Dateline—two to six lines below the last line of the printed letterhead.
  - The date should be written out in this form: January 1, 2012 or 1 January 2012
  - The date can be centered if letterhead is used.
  - If letterhead is not used, the date is included with the address of the writer.
- Reference line—a numerical file number, invoice number, policy number, or order numbers on a new line below the date.
- Special mailing notations—special notations such as "Confidential" two lines below the date.
- Inside address—the addressee's title and full name, business title, business name, and full address.
  - Do not abbreviate the company's name unless it is registered that way.
  - Cities and states should not be abbreviated.
  - Do not use "care of" before a hotel name or company name.
  - Include the appropriate title: *Mr., Ms., Mrs., Miss,* or *Dr.*
  - Business titles are never abbreviated.
- Attention line—one line space and the phrase "Attention:_____" after the inside address, if the letter is not addressed to any specific person.
  - You can make the letter go to the attention of a department.
  - An attention line is never used in a letter to an individual but only in a letter having plural addresses.
- Salutation—"Dear [person's name]," "Ladies and Gentlemen," "Dear Sir or Madam," "Dear [company name]" one line after the attention line or the inside address.

- ■ In business letters, the salutation is followed by a colon.
  - ■ In personal letters, the salutation is followed by a comma.
- ■ Subject line—an overview of what the letter is about.
  - ■ It can be used in place of a salutation.
  - ■ A subject line can be centered in sales letters.
  - ■ Do not include "Re" or "Subject" before the subject line.
  - ■ Underline the subject line, unless it occupies two or more lines, in which case underline the last line, letting the underline extend the length of the longest line in the subject.
- ■ Message—the body of your letter with paragraph breaks, optional indentions for paragraphs, bullet lists, and number lists.
- ■ Complimentary close—two lines below the last line of the message.
  - ■ The close is either left justified or five spaces to the right of center.
  - ■ "Yours truly" or "Very truly yours" can be used when no personal connection exists between the writer and recipient.
  - ■ "Sincerely" or "Sincerely yours" is appropriate when there is an established personal as well as business relationship.
  - ■ "Respectfully yours" is appropriate on letters addressed to a person of acknowledged authority.
  - ■ Avoid using closings such as "Yours for lower prices" or "I remain" or "Cordially yours."
- ■ Signature block—justified with the complimentary close with options of typed name and title, signature, or just signature.
  - ■ Never add a blank graphical line for the writer's signature.
  - ■ A woman should include a courtesy title in her typed signatures to allow the recipient of the letter to reply appropriately.

Example: Miss Louise A. Scott, Ms. Tina Anderson-Tate, Mrs. Pat Brueck

---

- ■ Identification initials—the initials of the typist aligned left two spaces below the signature block.
  - ■ Writer's initials are typed in capitals; the typist's initials are in lower case.

- A colon or slash is used to separate the initials.
- Enclosure notation—located with the identification initials or in place of them with the notation "enc," "encl," "enclosures (3)," or "3 encs."
- Copy notation—left-aligned two lines below identification initials with the notation "cc: [person's full name or initials]."
- Postscript—two spaces below the last text on the page with a "P.S." and then a short sentence.
  - Use a postscript to dramatize something already included in the letter.
  - Never use a postscript to include something that was forgotten during the writing of the letter. Instead, rewrite the letter.

Figure 15 Parts of a Business Letter

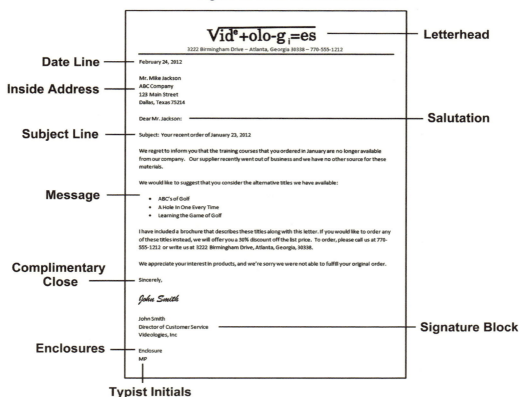

Business Letter Writing Style

Consider the following tips regarding business letter writing style:

- A good business letter advertises your capabilities and those of your company.
- A good business letter is neat and symmetrical, with no typographical, grammatical, or spelling errors.
- The language should be clear and simple.
- The first sentence should state the purpose of the letter.
- When responding to a letter, identify the subject and date of the previous letter in the first paragraph.
- Paragraphs should be short, and each paragraph should focus on a different topic.
- Use lists or italics where appropriate to make it easier for the reader to find important points.
- Focus on the reader's needs and interests.
- Avoid jargon.
- End with a call for action.

Example: Can we set up an appointment to discuss your needs on this project?

Business Letter Format

There are several different formats for business letters:

- Block letters (Figure 16)
- Modified block letters (Figure 17)
- Modified semiblock letters (Figure 18)
- Simplified letters (Figure 19)

(text continues on page 33)

Figure 16 Block Letter

5509 West 34th Street
Dallas, TX 75214
July 7, 2014

Michael J. Duffy
Intelligent Computer Systems
3121 Morris Lake Drive, Suite 211
Dallas, TX 75212

Dear Mr. Duffy,

I am writing to apply for the position you advertised in the Dallas Morning News for an e-learning developer. As you'll see in my résumé, I have the experience to fill this position.

For the past five years, I have been developing e-learning courses for three different companies: IBM, ATT, and Cox Enterprises. My experience has ranged from instructional design, technical writing, graphics production, multimedia production, and learning management system support.

Currently, I am working as a contractor for Cox Enterprises, where I am finishing a one-year assignment developing training for Oracle Financials. I have also recently developed documentation and training for PeopleSoft and for Hyperion Planning. I am currently the lead instructional designer on the Oracle Financials project that will conclude at the end of July.

Intelligent Computer Systems is famous for your innovative IT security systems and networking products. I would be proud to be part of the ICS team. I hope you will give me an opportunity to discuss my qualifications and experience. I can be reached at (214) 555-1212 after 6 p.m.

Thank you very much for your consideration for this position.

Sincerely yours,

Jeff Watkins
Jeff Watkins

Encl.: résumé

Figure 17 Modified Block Letter

5509 West 34th Street
Dallas, TX 75214
July 7, 2014

Michael J. Duffy
Intelligent Computer Systems
3121 Morris Lake Drive, Suite 211
Dallas, TX 75212

Dear Mr. Duffy,

I am writing to apply for the position you advertised in the Dallas Morning News for an e-learning developer. As you'll see in my résumé, I have the experience to fill this position.

For the past five years, I have been developing e-learning courses for three different companies: IBM, ATT, and Cox Enterprises. My experience has ranged from instructional design, technical writing, graphics production, multimedia production, and learning management system support.

Currently, I am working as a contractor for Cox Enterprises, where I am finishing a one-year assignment developing training for Oracle Financials. I have also recently developed documentation and training for PeopleSoft and for Hyperion Planning. I am currently the lead instructional designer on the Oracle Financials project that will conclude at the end of July.

Intelligent Computer Systems is famous for your innovative IT security systems and networking products. I would be proud to be part of the ICS team. I hope you will give me an opportunity to discuss my qualifications and experience. I can be reached at (214) 555-1212 after 6 p.m.

Thank you very much for your consideration for this position.

Sincerely yours,

Jeff Watkins
Jeff Watkins

Encl.: résumé

Figure 18 Modified Semiblock Letter

5509 West 34th Street
Dallas, TX 75214
July 7, 2014

Michael J. Duffy
Intelligent Computer Systems
3121 Morris Lake Drive, Suite 211

Dallas, TX 75212

Subj.: E-learning developer position

Dear Mr. Duffy,

I am writing to apply for the position you advertised in the Dallas Morning
News for an e-learning developer. As you'll see in my résumé,
I have the experience to fill this position.

    For the past five years, I have been developing e-learning courses for
three different companies: IBM, ATT, and Cox Enterprises. My experience
has ranged from instructional design, technical writing, graphics
production, multimedia production, and learning management system
support.

    Currently, I am working as a contractor for Cox Enterprises, where I am
finishing a one-year assignment developing training for Oracle Financials.
I have also recently developed documentation and training for PeopleSoft
and for Hyperion Planning. I am currently the lead instructional designer
on the Oracle Financials project that will conclude at the end of July.

    Intelligent Computer Systems is famous for your innovative IT security
systems and networking products. I would be proud to be part of the ICS
team. I hope you will give me an opportunity to discuss my qualifications
and experience. I can be reached at (214) 555-1212 after 6 p.m.

    Thank you very much for your consideration for this position.

Sincerely yours,

Jeff Watkins
Jeff Watkins

Encl.: résumé

Figure 19 Simplified Letter

July 7, 2014
5509 West 34th Street
Dallas, TX 75214

Subj.: E-learning developer position

I am writing to apply for the position you advertised in the Dallas Morning
News for an e-learning developer. As you'll see in my résumé, I believe
I have the experience to fill this position.

For the past five years, I have been developing e-learning courses for
three different companies: IBM, ATT, and Cox Enterprises. My experience
has ranged from instructional design, technical writing, graphics
production, multimedia production, and learning management system
support.

Currently, I am working as a contractor for Cox Enterprises, where I am
finishing a one-year assignment developing training for Oracle Financials.
I have also recently developed documentation and training for PeopleSoft
and for Hyperion Planning. I am currently the lead instructional designer
on the Oracle Financials project that will conclude at the end of July.

Intelligent Computer Systems is famous for your innovative IT security
systems and networking products. I would be proud to be part of the ICS
team. I hope you will give me an opportunity to discuss my qualifications
and experience. I can be reached at (214) 555-1212 after 6 p.m.

Thank you very much for your consideration for this position.

Sincerely yours,

Jeff Watkins
Jeff Watkins

Encl.: résumé

BUSINESS PLAN

A **business plan** is a proposal for new business or a strategy for expanding an existing business. A business plan includes (Figure 20):

■ A detailed description of the product or service.

■ Technical background information that explains the technologies involved.

■ A discussion of the market for the new product or service, including how it compares to existing products and services currently available.

    ■ The sales of comparison products or services are listed along with projected sales of the new product or service.

    ■ The differences between the new product or service and existing similar products or services are detailed.

■ The day-to-day operations of the business, including information about how the product or service is produced.

■ Facilities and personnel that the business will require.

■ Project revenues, along with supporting material for how the revenues projections were calculated.

■ Funding requirements to get the business started.

■ Legal issues involving competitors or government agencies.

■ A feasibility section discussing the likelihood of success and the overall investment potential of the business.

■ Investment documentation that details the amounts required for shareholder purchase.

The overall elements of the business plan document include:

■ Cover sheet

■ Statement of purpose

■ Table of contents

■ Description of the business

- Marketing information

- Competition

- Operating procedures

- Personnel

- Business insurance requirements

- Capital equipment and supply list

- Revenue projections

- Investment requirements

- Copies of résumés of all principals.

(text continues on page 42)

Figure 20 Business Plan

STEWART LAKE STATE PARK BUSINESS PLAN

Submitted to:

Department of Natural Resources

Division of Parks and Recreation

Office of the Director

Prepared for the Director by:

Stewart Lake State Park Superintendent

and

Division of Parks and Recreation Budget Officer

Division of State Parks and Recreation

(Courtesy of the U.S. Department of Natural Resources)

(continues)

Figure 20 *(continued)*

EXECUTIVE SUMMARY/INTRODUCTION

The purpose of the business plan is to assist park management and staff at Stewart Lake State Park in making decisions regarding the management, operation, and development of park resources. This plan focuses on the financial impacts of management decisions. Information from this document will be used to inform State park management and State legislators of financial impacts at Stewart Lake State Park.

MISSION, VISION, VALUES, AND OBJECTIVES

The mission, vision, values, and objectives of Stewart Lake State Park are as follows:

Mission
Enhance the quality of life through outdoor recreation, leisure, and educational experiences.

Vision
Provide quality outdoor recreational experiences through camping, boating, fishing, biking, hiking, and off-highway vehicle (OHV) trails.

Values
Meeting customer needs; innovation; clean and well-maintained facilities; preservation of natural surroundings and resources; affordable, safe, and accessible recreational activities.

Objectives
1. Increase overnight camping revenue (number of visitors and nights stayed)
2. Increase day-use revenues and visitation
3. Increase fishing activities and revenues

PARK DESCRIPTION AND STRENGTHS, WEAKNESSES, OPPORTUNITIES, AND THREATS

Description

Stewart Lake State Park was established in 1972, 2 years after the Bureau of Reclamation built the reservoir as part of the Strawberry-Duchesne River Project. The reservoir is located off of Highway 40, next to the city of Duchesne (population 5,000), 1½ hours east of Salt Lake City and 6 hours from Denver, Colorado. Highway 40 is a main corridor from Denver to Salt Lake City. The reservoir has over 23 miles of sandy shoreline and rests at approximately 5700 feet above sea level. Many of its formations and geologic features are similar to Lake Powell, but with a shorter "warm season" limiting peak visitation to the summer months (late June to early September).

The park provides for a variety of experiences with six campgrounds and open "boat camping" on many of its shores.

Market Analysis

Stewart Lake State Park's primary customers are boaters form the Wasatch Front area and anglers throughout the State and neighboring States. Current demand is primarily for improved access and regress for boats and improved facilities (hookups, docks, camping, etc.).

Demographics

The makeup of the population that recreates at Stewart Lake State Park is identified in the following table.

Summary of Demographic Information

Demographic	Local	State	National	International
Population	1,932,967	2,550,063	296,410,404	6,451,392,455
Average age	28.4	28.5	36.4	26.9
Income	$74,078	$47,934	$46,242	N/A
Male	50.1%	50.1%	49%	50.4%
Female	49.9%	49.9%	51%	49.6%

(continues)

Figure 20 *(continued)*

Market Trends

General trends in outdoor recreation are as follows:

- Greater awareness of value of leisure—overall increased demand for leisure activities.

- Expectation of recreation facilities—more "comfort" oriented.

- Preference for individual or informal activities is increasing. People are looking for "experiences."

- Participation by older adults in active recreation and sport has increased.

- Average age of outdoor recreation participant is increasing (baby boomers).

- Number of minority participants is increasing (most notably the Hispanic community).

Market Needs/Demands

The following needs and demands have been identified by park staff based on visitor feedback, trend analysis, and community comments for Stewart Lake State Park.

1. More, larger campsites/hookups for recreational vehicles (RVs)

2. Larger or additional boat ramp

3. Additional fish-cleaning stations (improve existing)

4. Added roads and "turn-around" for boat launching

5. Expanded parking for boats and day users

6. Protected docks (breakwater wall/marina)

7. Improve/expand bathrooms and showers

8. Expand "sandy" beach area for day users

9. Fuel station for boats

10. Improved bathrooms/showers at Knight Hollow and Indian Bay

11. More "accessible" water; expand culinary water system

12. Connect OHV trails to system outside of park

13. Improve OHV trails inside park

14. Develop group site for Knight Hollow (OHV users)

15. Add paved and non-paved trails for hiking and biking; link to city of Duchesne

16. Emphasize partnership with local businesses for food, rentals, and supplies—no concessionaire

17. Develop comfort camping facilities (i.e., yurts, cabins)

Financial Analysis

The division staff evaluates potential projects, programs, events, etc., using return on investment (ROI) (the ratio of **money** gained or lost on an **investment** relative to the amount of money invested) and payback period as its methods to measure the acceptability of each project. For long-term capital projects, internal rate of return (IRR) (the annualized effective compounded return rate which can be earned on the invested capital, i.e., the **yield** on the investment) and/or net present value (NPV) measures the excess or shortfall of cash flows, in **present value** (PV) terms, once financing charges are met. By definition, net present value cash flow methods are used. As a standard of acceptability, project ROI must meet or exceed the current State Treasurer's money market fund. Capital project IRR uses a hurdle rate of 3 percent and payback period of 30 years, or the estimated life of the structure/facility, whichever is less. It should be noted, however, that certain projects may be accepted even if the minimum criteria are not met based on such factors as environmental justice, safety, resource protection, heritage preservation, or division objectives.

(continues)

Figure 20 *(continued)*

The following tables are a financial summary of the proposed plan.

Financial Summary of Proposed Plan

Investment summary strategy description	Net cash flow ($)	Initial Investment ($)	Pay-back[1]	ROI (%)	IRR (%)	NPV[2] ($)
Mountain View Alternative 2	$239,160	$4,666,000	20	5.13	3.04	$145,000
Indian Bay	26,310	579,000	22	4.54	2.13	(50,000)
Rabbit Gulch	25,300	434,000	17	5.83	4.07	75,000
Juniper Point	16,450	278,000	17	5.92	4.19	53,000
Knight Hollow	10,825	194,000	18	5.58	3.71	24,000
Strawberry River Above	(165)	38,000	-230	-0.43	-0.43	(41,000)
Strawberry River Below	125	43,000	344	0.29	-11.65	(40,000)
Special events	2,950	3,000	1	98.33	—	—
Marketing	—	6,000	0	0.00	0.00	(6,000)
TOTAL	$320,955	$6,241,000	19	—	—	$160,000

[1] Payback is in years.
[2] Based on a 30-year life (except for special events and marketing).

Summary of Annual Funding Sources

Revenue type	Current ($)	Proposed ($)	Net effect ($)
General funds	$103,095	$364,765	$261,670
10% of total incremental revenue	28,252	68,572	40,320
Federal funds	0	0	0
Grants	0	0	0
Restricted funds (law enforcement)	86,300	86,300	0
Other funding sources	250	250	0
TOTAL REVENUES	$217,897	$519,887	$301,990

Summary of Annual Expenses

Expense type	Current ($)	Proposed ($)	Net Effect ($)
Wages and benefits	$183,052	$336,872	$153,820
Operating suppies/maintence	4,970	88,890	83,920
Utilities	10,425	23,725	13,300
Other costs (contractor/professional services)	2,250	9,600	7,350
Overhead	17,200	60,800	43,600
TOTAL EXPENSES	$217,897	$519,987	$301,990

Success Monitoring

The performance measures in the following table will be used to monitor and measure the success of the implementation of the above-mentioned strategies.

Performance Measures

Goal	Action Item	Measure Description	Target Score or Range
Meet or exceed projected visitor use levels identified for camping, cabins, pavilions, boating, and day use	Promote new facilities as they are brought on line	Match or exceed projected revenues	Maintain or exceed projected use for 3 years
Organize and hold a fishing derby	Establish partnership with agencies, clubs, associations, and promoters	Schedule and follow through on a fishing derby	Hold an event each year for 3 years
Organize and hold a half triathlon	Establish partnership with agencies, clubs, associations, and promoters	Schedule and follow follow through on a triathlon	Hold an event each year for 3 years

COLLECTION LETTER

Collection letters are written to collect amounts owed on a past-due account. When writing a collection letter, consider the following tips (Figure 21):

- Gather all the facts about the customer's account.

- Be specific about the amount owed and the date the funds were due.

- Let the customer know what the penalty will be if he or she fails to pay by a specific deadline.

  Example: If your payment is not received by November 1, 2012, your account will be sent to a collection agency.

- Offer assistance for customers having difficulty paying. Discuss new terms or a payment plan.

- If you must cancel a customer's credit, explain your reasons for doing so.

- Be courteous, but firm.

Collections letters are typically written to:

- Remind a customer that a payment is past due.

- Demand payment for a delinquent account.

- Inform a customer that legal action will be taken for failure to pay.

- Appeal to a customer to settle an account.

- Inform a customer of new business terms due to their failure to pay.

- Offer a customer a payment plan.

Figure 21 Collection Letter

AMC Corporation
1322 Westfield Lane
Los Angeles, CA 90025
September 21, 2014

Kenneth Barrymore
Eastern Distribution Company
41 West Mountain Highway
Denver, Colorado 80012

Dear Mr. Barrymore:

We currently have three outstanding invoices past the 30-day due date
for your account. These invoices are itemized below. All of these invoices
carry 30-day terms that were agreed upon in our distribution agreement,
and two of these invoices are over 90 days past due.

Invoice Number	Date	Amount
31431	05/22/2011	$2,134.99
31523	06/15/2011	$3,332.21
31731	08/01/2011	$2,451.31

We would appreciate your prompt payment by October 1, 2011;
otherwise, we will be forced to turn over your account to a collection
agency. In the meantime, any additional orders you make will have to
be on a cash-only basis until your account is paid in full.

Sincerely yours,

Albert Dayton

Albert Dayton
Accounts Receivable Manager
AMC Corporation

COMMENDATION LETTER

Commendation letters are often written to praise an employee's performance. Praise is a powerful motivator if it is genuine, specific, and timely. When writing a commendation letter, consider the following tips (Figure 22):

- Describe the work or accomplishment that deserves the commendation.
    - Use phrases such as "congratulations," "exceptional job," "very impressed," "must compliment you," "fine job," "outstanding success," "excellent quality," "professional manager," "your contribution," "positive impact."
- Describe the person's qualities that make him or her successful.
    - Use words such as *competence, expertise, diligence, commitment, enthusiastic, contribution, willingness, dedication, professional, extra time and effort, pride, invaluable, initiative, talent, leadership, ability.*
- Thank the person for his or her contribution to the organization.
    - Use phrases such as "job well done," "commend you," "vital to our success," "an asset to our company," "continued success," "further recognition," "thank you," "keep up the good work," "best wishes," "made the difference."

Commendation letters are typically written to:

- Praise an employee's performance.
- Compliment an employee from another organization.
- Praise a product or service.
- Compliment a guest speaker.
- Praise a salesperson from a supplier.
- Praise a chairperson or meeting planner.
- Compliment an instructor.
- Praise an employee's family for the employee's success.

Figure 22 Commendation Letter

Best Value Realty Company
4413 Lake Forest Drive
Woodstock GA 30189
October 22, 2012

Jack Moyer
1442 Pine Cliff Tarn
Woodstock, GA 30189

Dear Jack:

I wanted to congratulate you for achieving one million dollars in total sales this year.

In the history of Best Value Reality Company, we've only had two agents achieve this lofty goal. I would like to commend you for joining this elite group.

Your dedication in making cold calls, your helpful attitude when talking with homeowners, and your ability to help homeowners and buyers reach an agreement have all assisted you in achieving this outstanding success.

I want you to know that your efforts are vital to the success of Best Value Realty Company. You are indeed an asset to our company. Keep up the good work.

Sincerely yours,

Sherry Morgan

Sherry Morgan
President

COMPLAINT LETTER

Complaint letters are written to voice your opinion about something or to let a business know about an unsatisfactory situation. Remember, most errors are unintentional and most businesses want their customers to be satisfied.

When writing a complaint letter, consider the following tips (Figure 23):

- Write your complaint letter to a specific person at the organization, such as the manager, owner, or CEO.
- Write the letter with a positive tone without emotional language or obscenities.
- Keep the letter short, honest, and straightforward without omitting any relevant details.
- Send copies of any accompanying documentation and retain all the originals.
- Do not threaten or make generalizations about the organization.
- If other people you know were also affected by the problem, get multiple signatures on the complaint letter.
- Suggest a solution for the problem without destroying the relationship.
- Include your contact information including your name, address, phone number, and email address.

Complaint letters are typically written to:

- Complain about the quality of a product or service.
- Complain to governmental authorities.
- Complain to a landlord or neighbor.
- Complain about a billing problem.
- Complain about harassment at work.
- Complain to the news media.
- Complain about an order delay.
- Complain about an invoice.
- Reprimand an employee.
- Request a refund.
- Disagree with a coworker.

Figure 23 Complaint Letter

Leon Williams
14 Candler Avenue
Atlanta, GA 30311

August 8, 2014

Best Computers and Peripherals
32134 North 33rd Avenue
Tulsa, Oklahoma 74102

Gentlemen:

This letter is in reference to an Epson NX515 printer that I purchased online from your company on August 5, 2014. When the order arrived, the box contained an Epson NX415 printer.

While both printers are all-in-one printers, the NX515 has wireless networking capability, while the NX415 does not. There is also a price difference of $45.

I am enclosing a copy of my original online order for your reference.

I would like to return the Epson NX415 and exchange it for the Epson NX515 that I originally ordered. I would like for Best Computers and Peripherals to either send me a prepaid return authorization shipping label or reimburse me for the return shipping cost.

Earlier today, I checked your Web site which said the Epson NX515 is out-of-stock. The Web site did not say this last week when I placed my order. If you are unable to ship an Epson NX515, then I will keep the NX415, but I would like you to credit my credit card for the price difference of $45.

Sincerely yours,

Leon Williams

Leon Williams
(918) 555-6666
Lwilliams123@videologies.com

COVER LETTERS

Cover letters are often sent along with a résumé to emphasize what you can contribute to the hiring organization. When writing a cover letter, consider the following tips (Figure 24):

- Customize the letter for each job.

- Don't use a generic cover letter for every job application.

- Highlight your skills in bold font that match the job description.

- Make sure the cover letter does not contain any typos or grammatical mistakes.

- List specific examples of things you've accomplished and how each corresponds to the job description.

- Market your strengths, achievements, work ethic, and personality traits that will benefit the organization.

- Ask for an opportunity to interview.

Cover letters are typically written to:

- Respond to an advertisement for employment.

- Respond to a request for your résumé.

- Network with contacts during a job search.

- Accompany a proposal, report, or application.

- Respond to a job offer.

Figure 24 Cover Letter

12345 Heartside Drive
Western Branch, GA 31234
December 2, 2014

Mr. Kevin Wilson
President
Videologies, Inc.
10 North Main Street
Atlanta, GA 30303

Dear Mr. Wilson,

I am very interested in applying for the job of office assistant listed in the Atlanta Constitution on December 1.

As you can see from my enclosed résumé, I have worked for both a still photographer and a small video production company. I enjoyed working at both of these companies, and I feel this past experience qualifies me for the position described in your advertisement.

I have a good understanding of the visual medium and the many details you must handle in your work. I believe I can help take responsibility for some of these details with little additional training.

I would appreciate the opportunity for a personal interview. You can reach me at (770) 555-1234.

Thank you for your consideration.

Sincerely yours,

Evelyn Boyd
Evelyn Boyd

Encl.: résumé

DIRECTIVES

Directives are memos or emails that give instructions for a task, project, assignment, or new procedure. Directives address a particular problem and indicate a solution.

When writing directives, consider the following tips (Figure 25):

- State the reason for the directive, including a legislative compliance requirement, if any.

- Include specific instructions on what the reader is expected to do.

- State deadlines for the task or project.

- List any benefits that will be achieved from following the instructions detailed in the directive.

- Include the names and contact information for any resources who can answer questions or assist employees in implementing the directive.

- Thank the reader, and express confidence that the task or project can be completed.

Directives are typically written to:

- Establish new policies or procedures.

- Notify employees of a change in policy or procedure.

- Announce a special project.

- Issue instructions regarding a specific task or project.

- Delegate responsibility.

- Adjust territories or organizational structure.

Figure 25 Directive

ANNOUNCEMENT

To: All Employees

Effective January 1, 2012, new guidelines will go into effect for the use of contractors and consultants.

A written contract must be executed with all contractors and consultants and must include the following:

- A definition of the services to be performed;

- The fees to be charged to the company or the method of charging the company for the services; and

- The length of time the services will be provided.

These guidelines apply to any contractor or consultant currently performing services and to those that may be retained in the future. I have approved contracts that I can share and will be glad to customize them for specific circumstances you may have.

Please send me a copy of your signed contracts with contractors and consultants, so that I can maintain the agreements in a central location and track contract expiration and compliance.

Finally, these new guidelines establish the dollar limits for approval. For contracts for fewer than 90 days and less than $25,000, a director may approve the contract. For contracts for more than 90 days or more than $25,000, a vice president must approve the contract. Please ensure that the appropriate approval is obtained prior to engaging a contractor or consultant.

Thank you for your attention to these guidelines. If you have any questions, please let me know.

Edward Gibson
Vice President

EMAIL

Email is used in many businesses as a substitute for memos and brief telephone calls. Short messages are sent to request information, to share information, and to provide progress reports. When writing email messages, consider the following tips:

- When sending a message to a group of people, use the BCC field to keep everyone's email address private.
- Include a meaningful subject line.
    - Avoid starting a message with *Re*.
    - Capitalize your subject like a book title.

      Example: ISS Meeting on Tuesday

- Mark a message *urgent* or *high priority* only when it really is time sensitive.
- Include a personal greeting.

  Example: Hello Jim,

- Keep your message short and limited to one subject.
    - Send a separate email if you need to discuss a different subject.
- Avoid sending long documents as email messages.
    - Instead send attachments that have been compressed using a program like WinZip or Stuffit.
    - If sending an attachment, explain what the attachment is within the email message.
- The formatting of a message may change when viewed by the recipient.
    - Internal messages in HTML format may hold their formatting.
        - With internal HTML format messages, you can use bold, italics, underlining, multiple fonts, bullets, special symbols, tabs, and spacing to indent paragraphs.
    - External messages should avoid special formatting.

■ Email messages may include hyperlinks to World Wide Web addresses.

    ■ Use the entire address, including the Internet protocol.

    Example: http://www.videologies.com

■ Use the active rather than passive voice in your messages.

    Example of passive: Documents were drafted by the committee.

    Example of active: The committee drafted documents.

■ Avoid sexist language.

    Example: salesperson instead of salesman

■ If you make a request in your message, say "please."

■ Avoid all capital letters in your messages unless it is a warning like "DANGER."

■ When replying to an email, send a copy of the previous message or use a few lines as a quote.

    ■ For selective quoting, mark the previous message by using two << (less than) and two >> (greater than) symbols on each side of the quote.

    ■ Type your message below the quote or copy.

■ Like a business letter, include a formal signoff.

■ Include a signature (which can be stored as a signature file) with your messages.

    ■ Include your name, company, email address, phone number, and Web site.

    ■ Do not include pictures in your signature.

■ Always read and spell-check your messages before you send them.

The following are examples of when email is an inappropriate medium for communication:

- Thank-you notes
- Long memos
- Yes-or-no answers (use the phone instead)
- Job praise (offer it in person or in a letter)
- Telling your boss you are sick (on the phone instead)
- Requests for raises, promotions, or resignations (meet in person or write a letter)
- Jokes
- Flirting
- Gossip

ENDORSEMENT LETTER

An **endorsement letter** is used to endorse a candidate for an award, to endorse a political candidate, or to endorse a person for a particular position. When writing an endorsement letter, consider the following tips (Figure 26):

- Include your name and organization and your relationship with the person being endorsed.
- Describe what you are endorsing and why.
  - Explain why the person is entitled to your endorsement.
  - List how long you've known the person.
  - List the person's qualities.
- Explain what this person will do in the future, given his or her skills and qualities.
- Include your contact information if the reader needs additional information.
- Conclude by restating your endorsement.

Endorsement letters are typically written to:

- Advocate legislation.
- Endorse a candidate.
- Endorse a person for a job.
- Endorse a nominee for an award.
- Endorse a product or service.
- Confirm a decision made by someone else.
- Endorse a report.
- Confirm authorization given to someone to act on your behalf.
- Endorse a business.

Figure 26 Endorsement Letter

May 10, 2012

Laura Johnson
1322 Flowering Field Circle
Roswell, GA 30123

Office of Admissions
Candler School of Theology
Emory University
Atlanta, GA 30322

Dear Emory University,

I am writing in regards to Darlene Williams, who has applied for admission to the Candler School of Theology. I have been asked to provide a work or character reference.

First of all, I would like to strongly recommend your acceptance of Darlene. She is a very talented, smart, and spiritual being. Wherever this path leads, it will surely be a blessing for those who come into contact with her in the future.

(continues)

Figure 26 *(continued)*

I have known Darlene both personally and professionally for over 12 years. She has worked for my company on numerous occasions as a professional on-camera presenter. She is one of the best in her field.

Over the years, I have become friends with Darlene and have discussed her past and present religious beliefs. Darlene grew up in Asheville, North Carolina, on a small farm where her parents still live. Her parents are active in the church and taught Darlene to pray, have faith, and be kind to others. I see the result today as someone who "shines."

While Darlene considers herself a Christian, she is accepting of other ideas and beliefs. She knows there is more to life than just following the dance steps to salvation. This was demonstrated recently, when she was counseling a woman at her church regarding the death of a loved one. The woman was afraid her dead husband wasn't going to heaven because he might have violated some of the belief system rules for obtaining salvation. Darlene told this woman something that summarizes why Darlene shines. She said, "People sometimes tend to underestimate the size of God's love."

If we jump into the future and listen to Darlene a few years from now after graduating from the Candler School of Theology, I'm sure I'll hear something just as comforting. Darlene's unique experience as an on-camera presenter, public speaker, and trainer, combined with the insights and knowledge acquired from this educational experience, should result in someone who not only communicates, but also counsels, heals, and inspires.

I'm excited that Darlene has chosen this path and has chosen to further her knowledge and spiritual growth by applying to Emory University. It is something to celebrate, a chance to see destiny fulfilled.
Sincerely,

Laura Johnson

Laura Johnson

FORMS

Business forms are created for common fill-in-the-blank documents such as job applications, health benefit claims, and legal documentation.

For legal documents, write numbers in words and then repeat them immediately in numerals inside parentheses.

Example: ten thousand five hundred and seventy-five (10,575)

For dates in legal forms, the month is always spelled out.

The following words and phrases often used in legal documents (Figure 3.27) are customarily written in full capitals, usually followed by a comma, a colon, or no punctuation:

- THIS AGREEMENT, made this second day of . . .

- KNOW ALL MEN BY THESE PRESENT, that . . .

- IN WITNESS WHEREOF, I have this day . . .

- MEMORANDUM OF AGREEMENT made this twenty-fifth day of . . .

Case titles in legal documents are always underscored, followed by a comma, the volume and page numbers, and date.

Example: Johnson v. Smith, 201 Okla. 433, 32 Am. Rep. 168 (1901).

Notary public forms are used to acknowledge and witness document signatures (Figures 28–30).

Figure 27 Contract

THIS AGREEMENT, made this _____day of _____, 20____,
between _____ of _____ , First Party (hereinafter
called the Seller), and _____a corporation under the laws of the
State of _____, with principal place of business in _____,
_____(city and state), Second Party (hereinafter called the
Purchaser).

WITNESSETH:

WHEREAS the Seller has this day agreed to _____; and
WHEREAS the Purchaser is willing to _____; and
WHEREAS_____; NOW, THEREFORE, it is agreed that
_____. WITNESS the signatures of the parties hereto on the
date aforesaid.

(S)_____
Seller

(S)_____
Purchaser

By_____
President

[Corporate Seal]

Figure 28 Notary Form for an Individual

For an individual
State of _____
County of _____
On the ____ day of _____, 20___, before me came _____
known to me to be the individual described in and who executed the fore-
going instrument and acknowledged that he (or she) executed the same.

(S)_____
Notary Public

[Stamp and Seal]

Figure 29 Notary Form for a Corporation

For a corporation

State of _____

County of _____

On the _____ day of _____, 20___, before me personally appeared _____to me known, who, being by me duly sworn, did depose and say that he (or she) resides at _____; that he (or she) is _____(title) of _____(Company), the corporation described in and which executed the foregoing instrument; that he (or she) knows the seal of said corporation; that the seal affixed to said instrument is such corporate seal; that it was so affixed by order of the (title) of said corporation; and that he (or she) signed his (or her) name thereto by like order.

(S)_____

Notary Public

[Seal]

Figure 30 Notary Form for a Partnership

For a partnership

State of _____

County of _____

On the _____ day of _____, 20___, before me personally appeared _____ to me known, and known to me to be a member of _____ (name of partnership), and the person described in and who executed the foregoing instrument in the firm name of _____, and he (or she) duly acknowledged to me that he (or she) executed the same as and for the act and deed of said firm of _____ (repeat name of partnership).

(S)_____

Notary Public

[Seal]

FUND-RAISING LETTER

Fund-raising letters are written by nonprofit organizations, schools, civic organizations, and clubs to raise money from donors. When writing a fund-raising letter, consider the following tips (Figure 31):

- Use a personal and conversational tone.

- Introduce yourself and the organization, and thank readers for their support and interest in the organization.

- Describe the cause and credentials of the organization.

  - Explain the critical need, what the organization has accomplished in the past, and how the requested funds would be used.

- Ask for a specific donation amount and explain how that donation will help the organization.

  - Explain how donations of this amount have helped the organization in the past.

  - Specifically mention any previous donations from the person.

- Optionally, offer an incentive for a donation such as a tangible gift or a perceived value.

Example: Imagine the impact your donation of $100 will have on the lives of ten children in rural India.

- Optionally, include a separate page or a brochure with detailed information about the program and fund-raising campaign.

  - Include photographs statistics, and the budget.

- Thank readers for their generosity.

- Conclude the letter by leaving a positive feeling about the needy cause.

- The letter should be personally signed by someone from the organization.

Fund-raising letters are typically to:

- Request a donation.

- Invite someone to attend a fund-raising event.

- Thank someone for a donation.

- Announce a new fund-raising campaign.
- Inform members of the financial needs of the organization.
- Introduce a new program offered by the charitable organization.

Figure 31 Fund-Raising Letter

September 12, 2012

Hopewell Middle School
131 Westfield Place
Kansas City, MO 67511

Alice Johnson
83 Cambridge Drive
Kansas City, MO 67511

Dear Mrs. Johnson:

As president of the Hopewell Middle School Parent Teachers Association, I want to thank you for your support last year. Involved parents like you are what help make Hopewell a great school and allow us to work as an effective PTA that supports the efforts of the teachers and staff.

For this new school year, Hopewell has been forced by the school district to reduce its operating budget by ten percent, which has resulted in layoffs of our art and music teachers. As a result, the PTA is now actively engaged in a campaign to raise funds to help the school hire at least one part-time art teacher and one part-time music teacher. Our goal is to raise $30,000 for the year through a variety of fund-raising efforts.

To start this effort, we are asking our PTA members to make a donation of $100 if at all possible. If you and other parents can contribute this amount, that will help us raise nearly one-third of our goal. That would allow the school to hire these part-time teachers. Additional fund-raising would be needed to cover their salaries through the end of the school year.

(continues)

Figure 31 *(continued)*

The value of including art and music education is extremely important in helping our children develop their cultural talents. As a community, we would be remiss to disregard this need and allow budget cuts to reduce the quality of the education our children receive.

I hope you'll join me and the rest of the PTA members in making this first step toward a successful 2012 at Hopewell Middle School.

Sincerely yours,

Carol Masters

Carol Masters
PTA President

GRANT PROPOSALS

A **grant proposal** should include the following elements (Figure 32):

- Cover letter
  - An introduction to the organization requesting the grant
  - A summary of the proposal
  - A summary of any previous communications with the funding organization
  - The amount of funding you are requesting
  - The population that will be served by the grant
  - The need the project will help solve
- Cover page
  - Grant proposal title
  - Submitted to: (funding organization's name)
  - Date
  - Your contact information including name, title, organization, address, phone, and email
- Proposal report

- The content and format, varying depending on the requirements of the funding organization

A basic grant proposal should include the following sections:

- Project abstract or summary—a concise summary of the project that is no longer than one page. Write this section of the proposal last.
  - Need for the project
  - Population served
  - Brief description of the project
  - Goals and objectives of the project
  - Applicant's history
  - How the program will be evaluated
- Statement of need
  - Description of the problem
  - Description of the population
  - Description of how the project will help solve the problem
- Goals and objectives
- Program description
  - Explanation of the program
  - Details on how the program will be implemented
  - Explanation of what will be accomplished
  - Timeline, the schedule for project implementation
- Evaluation—information on how the success of the project will be measured
- Organization and staff information
  - Description of the organization's experience
  - Staff qualifications
- Budget—a summary of the expenses for the project
- Appendix
  - Research support
  - Nonprofit tax status letter
  - Annual report

(text continues on page 70)

Figure 32 Grant Proposal

Date

Contact Person
Organization
Address
City, State, Zip

Dear _____,

Isha Foundation is a nonprofit 501(c)(3), international service organization that conducts various public welfare programs in parts of the world to advance physical and mental health. Isha Foundation is a volunteer organization funded with public and private assistance.

The Foundation's Action for Rural Rejuvenation (ARR) initiative is a comprehensive rural rehabilitation program that provides initial relief for urgent medical needs and ongoing services to restore inner well-being and rebuild communities in India. This project was launched in August 2003 with a mission to benefit 70 million rural people in 54,000 villages in Tamil Nadu, South India. It will be implemented in two phases over a period of 15 years. Thereafter, it is envisioned that local communities will sustain the project activities independently.

Currently, ARR operates nine Mobile Health Clinics (MHC) and provides services to 143,000 patients in 280 villages each year. Of these patients, 67,000 are elderly people, 87,000 are women, and 21,000 are children. Over 50% of the MHC patients suffer from chronic ailments such as ulcers, musculoskeletal disorders, hypertension, depression, and respiratory disorders including asthma. On average, each new MHC that is deployed can provide services for over 17,000 patients each year. Because rural children with conjunctivitis often scratch their eyes resulting in blindness, each MHC can provide timely medical services to over 2600 children each year. In addition to medical services for existing conditions, the staff on the MHCs offers preventive health care services in the form of yoga classes and provides sporting equipment to encourage physical activity.

ARR plans to launch 59 MHCs in the next three years, and 150 before the end of 2013. Isha Foundation is seeking funding to help us sustain and expand our ongoing ARR effort. Each MHC costs approximately $29,000 to purchase and equip. The yearly operating expenses for one MHC are approximately $17,000.

Isha Foundation is a nonreligious, nonpolitical, nonsectarian organization with over 250,000 active volunteers worldwide. Isha Foundation has over 150 centers in India and other parts of the world including the United States, Canada, Lebanon, Cyprus, France, and Germany. Based in Coimbatore, India, the foundation manages 87 centers in Tamil Nadu alone.

Over the past 14 years, Isha Foundation has successfully carried out several social outreach programs for rural people, as well as disadvantaged and often neglected segments of society, throughout Tamil Nadu, thereby gaining a reputable and trustworthy standing among the people throughout India.

Sincerely,
Your Name
Contact Information

(Courtesy of Isha Foundation)

ACTION FOR RURAL REJUVENATION

Submitted to: XYZ Foundation

October 10, 2014

Name
Isha Foundation
Address
Phone
Email

(continues)

Figure 32 *(continued)*

I. Summary

The Isha Foundation's Action for Rural Rejuvenation (ARR) initiative is a multi-pronged, multi-phased, holistic, outreach program whose primary objective is to improve the overall health and quality of life of the rural poor of India. ARR is a unique, well-defined philanthropic effort, which enhances existing development schemes by supporting indigenous models of health, prevention and community participatory governance, while offering primary health care services and allopathic treatment through its dedicated team of qualified and trained personnel.

At present, nearly 750,000 people in rural Tamil Nadu, India are served by Isha's ARR project. ARR features Mobile Health Clinics (MHC), which are able to traverse hard-to-reach regions and effectively operate in resource-poor environments.

In addition to medical services for existing conditions, the staff on the MHCs offers preventive health care services in the form of yoga classes and provides sporting equipment to encourage physical activity.

II. Statement of Need

Currently, ARR operates nine MHCs and provides services to 143,000 patients in 280 villages each year. Of these patients, 67,000 are elderly people, 87,000 are women, and 21,000 are children. Over 50% of the MHC patients suffer from chronic ailments such as ulcers, musculoskeletal disorders, hypertension, depression, and respiratory disorders including asthma.

On average, each new MHC that is deployed can provide services for over 17,000 patients each year. Because rural children with conjunctivitis often scratch their eyes resulting in blindness, each MHC can provide timely medical services to over 2600 children each year.

III. Goals and Objectives

This project was launched in August 2003, under the aegis of Isha Foundation. The project aims to benefit 70 million rural people in 54,000 villages in Tamil Nadu, South India. It will be implemented in two phases over a period of 15 years. Thereafter, it is envisaged that local communities will sustain the project activities independently.

The goals of Phase One include:

- Ensuring access to essential medical care by running mobile health clinics and distributing medicines free of cost

- Rejuvenating traditional well-being tools by introducing basic yogic practices

- Developing a sense of community involvement and joy by conducting games and inter-village tournaments

- Introducing the use of home remedies and herbs for cost effective and healthy living by providing free training and developing model herbal gardens

- Bringing awareness on preventive health, sanitation, and environmental conservation by conducting specially designed awareness programs

- Sustaining further development of the program by creating a local volunteer base

The goals of Phase Two of the project include building Rural Development Centers which will include a village library, computer center, yoga center, gymnasium, pharmacy, health clinic, and volleyball court. Phase Two will also include setting up contemporary crafts training and production units for economic development.

ARR plans to launch 59 MHCs in the next three years, and 150 before the end of 2013. Since Rural Development Centers (RDC) that are built in the second phase of the project will comprise a health clinic and pharmacy, the MHCs of the areas covered by these centers will be redirected to other regions. In villages where RDCs are not established or are remote, the MHC service will be sustained.

IV. Project Design and Implementation Plan

Central to the ARR project are the Mobile Health Clinics. These overcome two major barriers to appeasing existing illnesses: cost—by offering free examination and treatment; and access—by bringing the medical team to the rural people.
The MHCs are specially designed vehicles built on a conventional truck chassis incorporating all the built-in features of a clinic. They are outfitted with all common diagnostic equipment, a clinical laboratory, pharmacy, and an independent power and water supply. They are equipped so doctors can perform surgical treatments such as abscess draining, suturing, dressing, and childbirths. Immunizations for malaria and other diseases are provided. Whenever more complex care is needed, free medical examination and treatment or discounted fees and payment plans are negotiated at partnering local hospitals.

(continues)

Figure 32 *(continued)*

Each MHC includes a qualified allopathic physician, a trained nurse, two trained assistants and a pharmacist. The physicians are additionally trained in indigenous systems of healing. Prior to fieldwork, the MHC staff undergoes an intense training process including an orientation to working in resource-poor environments and guidance on how to effectively reach out and build rapport with the community in which they work.

In order to allow for maximal utilization of MHCs, standardized protocols have been implemented, including procedures for setup, data entry, and designations of roles and responsibilities of the staff. Apart from providing medical services, the MHC staff integrates with the local community. They share meals and reside in the homes of local villagers. Through these personal interactions, the MHC staff is better equipped to understand the needs and requirements of the local community. Furthermore, through these intimate interactions, they are able to ensure reciprocal dialogue with the community, mobilize support and by their example, inspire villagers to take responsibility for community health and well-being.

V. Timeline

Upon the funding of this grant request, a mobile health clinic can be purchased and equipped within three weeks. It can be on the road serving villages within one month.

Initially, a maximum of two villages are serviced daily by one MHC in order to assure adequate introductory and screening measures. Subsequently, a routine schedule is adopted during which each MHC typically services 4-5 villages daily, repeating these visits to each village on a fortnightly basis. Typically, one MHC serves 60-75 villages twice a month. Each clinic is in operation 24 days a month.

VI. Evaluation

The staff on each MHC maintains patient records, so the outcome of the project is easily measured in terms of number of patients served, the types of medical conditions treated, as well as demographic breakdown by age and sex.

For each MHC deployed, our target is to service 20,000 patients each year with a service area of approximately 60 rural villages.

VII. Organizational Capacity

Established in 1992, Isha Foundation is an international public service organization, founded by Jaggi Vasudev, dedicated to the enhancement of physical, mental and inner well-being of all people. Isha seeks to bring peace, inner balance and joy through the science of yoga and to relieve human suffering through a variety of initiatives on the individual, community and international level. Isha Foundation is a non-religious, non-political, non-sectarian organization with over 250,000 active volunteers worldwide.

Isha Foundation has over 150 centers in India and other parts of the world including the United States, Canada, Lebanon, Cyprus, France, and Germany. Based in Coimbatore, India, the foundation manages 87 centers in Tamil Nadu alone.

Isha is a predominantly volunteer-run organization. People who have been in some way touched and inspired by Isha Foundation comprise the volunteer base. Coming from all walks of life and all parts of the world, their quality of being dedicated, disciplined, and wanting to reach out is what is common across the organization.

Over the past 14 years, Isha Foundation has successfully carried out several social outreach programs for rural people, as well as disadvantaged and often neglected segments of society, throughout Tamil Nadu, thereby gaining a reputable and trustworthy standing among the people throughout India.

In addition to the selfless dedication of its volunteers, ARR is fueled and supported through its extensive partnerships with renowned national and international organizations, medical centers, and administrative centers, such as the Times Foundation, the Ramakrishna Hospitals, the Masonic Medical Center, the Kovai Medical Center Hospital, the KG Hospitals, the ELGI Group of Companies, and Shambhavi Trust, just to name a few. As part of their commitment to Action for Rural Rejuvenation, these organizations have pledged free and subsidized medical treatment to patients referred by the project, sponsored the design, construction or provision of the mobile health clinics and offered assistance of their own medical teams to go on rotation on the MHCs, among many other pledges.

(continues)

Figure 32 *(continued)*

VIII. Project Budget

We are seeking funding for:

One Mobile Health Clinic (MHC) Truck

Purchasing one additional MHC will allow Action for Rural Rejuvenation to serve up to 60 additional villages and as many 20,000 new patients the first year.

The cost for purchasing a MHC is $29,070.

While we can seek funding from other sources for the operating costs, the budget to operate the MCH for one year is an additional $17,442.

IX. Appendix

Attached are letters of support from our support organizations, such as the Times Foundation and the Kovia Medical Center Hospital, as well as our tax exempt status letter from the Internal Revenue Service.

INSTRUCTIONS

Instructions are step-by-step explanations of how to perform a particular procedure. Instructions are often written for product manuals, user guides, repair guides, and training manuals.

When writing instructions, consider the following guidelines (Figure 33):

- Instructions should be clear and written simply.
- The audience for the instructions should be clearly identified, and the instructions should be written to this audience's level of understanding.
- The instructions should have an introduction, listing:
  - Who should perform the procedure.
  - Any equipment, supplies, or documentation needed.
  - Special conditions or safety concerns, if any.
    - Warnings, cautions, and danger notices should alert readers of any possibility of hurting themselves or damaging equipment.

- Tasks involved in the procedure should be broken down into individual steps.
- Instruction steps should be numbered.
    - Substeps can be indented and alphabetized if they have to be performed in order.
    - If substeps can be performed in any order, bullets can be used.
- Supplementary information can provide commentary on what the process should look like at specific points in the instructions.
- Use the active voice for instructions.

Incorrect: The ENTER key should be pressed.

Correct: Press the ENTER key.

- Drawings, photographs, or screen captures are useful as roadmap illustrations.
- Major divisions of tasks can be grouped together under a heading.

Figure 33 Instructions

HOW TO ACCESS THE PRECLASS WEBINAR

Getting Started

Before attending the Technical Analysis class, you will need to sign in to the learning management system (LMS) and view a preclass webinar.

To access the LMS and view the webinar, you will need:

- The course password (tech123)

- Your employee identification number

- The Web address for the LMS: http://www.lms.com

You will need approximately one hour to view the webinar.

(continues)

Figure 33 *(continued)*

How to Find Your Employee ID

You will need your employee ID to sign in to the LMS. If you don't know your employee ID, follow these steps:

1. Open Internet Explorer and enter the following Web address: http://www.tech.com

2. Click the **Sign In** link in the top right corner.

3. On the Sign In page, change the Validation source to **Employee ID**.

4. New hyperlinks will be displayed. Click the link for **Forgot User ID**.

5. Answer the personal questions on the Verify Identity screen to get your employee ID.

Viewing the Preclass Webinar

Follow these steps to sign into the LMS and view the preclass Webinar:

1. Open Internet Explorer and enter the address for the LMS: http://www.lms.com

2. In the Quick Links section on the left side of the screen, click **Search Courses**.

3. On the Search Courses screen, select **Online Courses**; then click the **Go** button.

4. From the list of courses, select **TECH900**, and then click the **Select** button.

5. On the Sign On page, enter your employee ID and your last name as the password.

6. Click the **OK** button.

7. The preclass webinar will be displayed.

Warning: If you have a pop-up blocker running, the Webinar will not be displayed. To check, click the Internet Explorer **Tools** menu, then **Pop-Up Blocker**, and then check the setting. Make sure it is turned off.

INTRODUCTIONS

An **introduction** is usually the first section in a formal report. The introduction introduces the report to the reader.

The introduction explains what the report is about, why it was written, for whom it was written, and what it will cover. An introduction is usually no more than one or two pages (Figure 34).

Most introductions do the following:

- Introduce the topic of the report.

- Explain the purpose of the report.

- Identify the target audience for the report.

- Provide an overview of the content covered in the report.

- Provide any history that may motivate readers to be interested.

Sections within the report may have their own introductions. A section introduction introduces a new topic, provides a content overview of the topic, and eases the transitions between sections.

Figure 34 Introduction

INTRODUCTION

America's Dynamic Workforce presents an overview of current conditions and notable trends affecting the American labor market and economic activity. Primary emphasis is on measures of labor market performance—employment, labor force participation, unemployment, and compensation. General measures of economic performance such as gross domestic product (GDP) and productivity growth are also described as they relate to labor market conditions and trends. Throughout this report the focus is on the data—what the numbers actually say about the American labor market—and on how individual data items fit together to present an overall portrait of the health and dynamism of the market.

There are six chapters:

Chapter 1 summarizes the current levels and trends of payroll jobs, total employment, job openings, turnover, unemployment, and GDP.

Chapter 2 provides a global context for understanding the U.S. labor market and compares the United States and other countries along common dimensions of labor market indicators.

Chapter 3 presents an overview of patterns, recent trends and projections regarding the distribution of employment across industries and occupations.

Chapter 4 examines the educational attainment of the labor force, including trends and comparisons of employment, earnings, and unemployment relative to educational attainment.

(continues)

Figure 34 *(continued)*

Chapter 5 examines the concept of labor force flexibility in terms of schedules, work arrangements, and other factors.

Chapter 6 highlights the dimensions of opportunity in the American workforce, including dynamic age, gender, race, and ethnicity perspectives.

The end notes provide important technical details, caveats, and references to additional information about the data items discussed in the main text.

Most of the tables and charts in America's Dynamic Workforce: 2006 reflect annual average data for calendar years ending in 2005 as the most recent full year available. In some cases, monthly data through the latest available month in 2006 (typically June) are also referenced.

In this report, the terms "population" and "labor force" refer to the civilian non-institutional population ages 16 and older and to the civilian labor force age 16 and over unless specified otherwise. Similarly, data on workers refer to employed persons age 16 and over unless otherwise noted. Monthly or quarterly labor market data are seasonally adjusted unless specified otherwise.

Much of the data in this report were compiled from the public access files of the Bureau of Labor Statistics' Web site at www.bls.gov.

(Courtesy of the U.S. Department of Labor)

INQUIRY LETTER

Inquiry letters are written to ask for information or to make a request. Don't send an inquiry letter for information you could easily obtain on the Internet or on the telephone. Allow two weeks after sending an inquiry letter and not getting a response before sending a follow-up letter.

When writing an inquiry letter, consider the following tips (Figure 35):

- Use a courteous tone because you are requesting the reader's time to fulfill your request.

- Begin the letter by stating who you are and how you found out about the reader's organization.

- State what you are requesting as clearly as possible.

- Explain the purpose of your request and how it will help you.

  - Mention your qualifications, if doing so is appropriate.

- The letter should be short but should adequately explain what you are requesting and what action you want the reader to take.

- Offer to pay for any copies or supplies that might be needed to fulfill your request.

  - Provide a self-addressed stamped envelope if you have requested documents.

- Include the date you need the information.

- When the person responds to your inquiry, send a thank-you note.

Inquiry letters are typically written to:

- Request technical assistance.

- Request a reprinted article or publication.

- Seek personal advice.

- Request information about a product or service.

- Request an official document.

- Request a reply to a survey.

- Request an application.

- Request an estimate or bid.

- Request information about a job seeker.

- Request information from a government agency.

- Request samples or information.

Figure 35 Inquiry Letter

May 15, 2012

654 West Lake Drive
Seattle, WA 98101

Technical Support
First Data Software
421 Research Drive, Suite 300
Research Triangle Park, NC 27709

Dear Technical Support Department:

I am writing to ask some questions about First Data's new upgrade for Kitchen Designer 4.0. I have been using Kitchen Designer 2.0 in my remodeling business for the past several years and it has helped me immensely.

I've read the latest sales literature about the software, but I was unable to find the answers to my questions. Since the new version has not yet been released, your online support pages also do not answer my questions.

To upgrade, I need to know whether the new software will operate properly with my current computer. Please let me know the answers to the following:

1. Does Kitchen Designer 4.0 still use a serial port security dongle?

2. Will the software support a geForce 800 video card using twin monitors?

3. Will designs created using Kitchen Designer 2.0 open in 4.0?

If your answer to all three questions is "yes," then I would definitely be interested in purchasing the upgrade.

You can respond to me by email at lsullivan@abcd.com or by calling me at (206) 555-1111. I appreciate your assistance.

Sincerely,

Louis Sullivan

Louis Sullivan

JOB DESCRIPTIONS

Job descriptions are often used when advertising an open position or when determining compensation.

A job description focuses on the job responsibilities, tasks, key qualifications, and basic skills needed to perform the job (Figure 36).

The categories that make up a typical job description include:

■ Job title

■ Department and to whom the person directly reports

■ List of responsibilities

■ List of other job titles and departments that the person will work with on a regular basis

■ Terms of employment

■ The necessary skills and experience required, including length of previous experience, educational requirements, and certifications

For existing positions, focus on the future needs and objectives of the business rather than on the current responsibilities of the position.

Be specific when describing tasks and responsibilities.

Any references to race, color, religion, age, sex, national origin, nationality, or physical or mental disability are illegal.

Figure 36 Job Description

Title of the position
Training Project Manager

Department
Human Resources

Reports to
Manager of Learning Technology

Overall responsibility
Provides project management and training development services for learning management system implementations and upgrades

Key areas of responsibility

- Provide project management services for e-learning course development.
- Provide training services for LMS administrators at subsidiaries.
- Develop training for LMS administrators and users.
- Provide support services for LMS users.
- Produce distance learning Webinars for Benefits and PeopleSoft instruction.
- Provide support to subsidiaries for e-learning implementations on the LMS.
- Manage the LMS administrator.
- Process training requests and assignments.

Consults with

- Human Resources Development department
- Training departments at subsidiaries

Term of employment
Full-time, on-site, hours 8:00 A.M to 5:00 P.M.

Qualifications

- At least two years of project management experience for software implementations
- Experience working with learning management systems
- Experience conducting instructor-led training sessions
- Experience writing workbooks and job aids
- Experience supporting end users in a help desk function

JOB OFFER LETTER

Job offer letters are written by an employer to a job candidate to offer employment with the company.

Job offer letters should include facts about the following (Figure 37):

■ Starting salary

■ Job location

■ Working hours

■ Benefits

■ Start date

■ Job title

■ Job responsibilities

The tone of the letter should be direct and encouraging. The offer may be contingent on providing proof of employment eligibility.

Figure 37 Job Offer Letter

January 20, 2012

Communication Enterprises
3211 West Peachtree Street
Dunwoody, GA 32311

Aileen Robertson
2422 Churchill Lane, Apt 233
Roswell, GA 30322

Dear Ms. Robertson:

It is my pleasure to present our offer of employment as training developer, reporting to me, Ken Wallace, Learning Technology Manager.

As training developer, you will be creating course manuals, PowerPoint presentations, and Help systems as a part of your normal job. In addition, you may also be asked to serve as an instructor from time to time.

Your annualized base salary will be $62,000, payable on a semimonthly basis. You will also be eligible for an annual incentive, which will range from 0% to 4% of base salary paid, with a target of 3% of base salary paid.

Communication Enterprises offers the following competitive benefits, all of which are subject to the terms of the company or benefit plan guidelines. All of these benefits are covered in detail in the enclosed documents. You will be eligible to participate in the company health plan upon hire and in the company pension plan upon hire or at age 21, whichever is later. Based on your projected hire date of February 1, 2012, you will be eligible to participate in the 401(k) plan on July 1, 2012. Additionally, you will have up to two weeks of paid vacation, nine company paid holidays, and two personal floating holidays.

Aileen, you bring a background of experience and capability that should greatly enhance our efforts in the training department. We look forward to the beginning of a long and mutually rewarding relationship.

Sincerely,

Ken Wallace

Ken Wallace
Learning Technology Manager

MEETING AGENDA

A **meeting agenda** is a road map for a meeting. The agenda provides the plan for the meeting and a sense of direction and purpose.

A meeting agenda should include (Figure 38):

- Meeting starting and ending times
- Meeting location
- Topic headings with topic details
- How much time each topic discussion is expected to last
- Which meeting participants will facilitate the topics

Figure 38 Meeting Agenda

Meeting Called By:	Session #:	Date:	Starting Time:
Mark Rivers		1/28/2014	9:30 a.m.
Location:	**Dress Code (optional):**		**Ending Time:**
Central Park Conference Room 11a			12:00 p.m.
Meeting Objective and Scope:			
JAD Session—The Big Picture.			
Time	**Topic**		**Leader**
9:30–9:35	Welcome and review agenda.		Mark Rivers
9:35–9:55	Basic data flow for enrollments.		Ritva Porter
9:55–10:15	Ongoing data requirements		Ritva Porter
10:15–10:35	Basic data flow for pay processing		Ritva Porter
10:35–10:45	Break		
10:45–11:10	Basic data flow for 401(k) billing.		Ritva Porter
11:10–11:30	Basic data flow for termination processing.		Ritva Porter
11:30–11:50	Basic data flow for loans.		Ritva Porter
11:50–12:00	Wrapup		Mark Rivers
Facilitator:	**Time Keeper:**		**Scribe**
Ritva Porter			Debra Miller
Attendees:			

Anne Fried, Mark Rivers, Donna Morgan, Tonya Smith, Debra Miller, Sally Roberts, Susan Mullins, Ebony Hollings, Tanya Sanchez, Mary McKnight, Daphne Johnson, Mike Harper, Kevin Wilson, Kendall Williams, Rita Zezula, Darlene Price

MEETING MINUTES

Meeting minutes are a record of what took place during a meeting. They allow the meeting attendees to review the meeting later to look for outstanding issues and action items.

In some cases, such as stockholder and board of directors meetings, the minutes are required by law and are included in the corporate minute book.

Meeting minutes should include (Figure 39):

- The name of organization

- The name of body conducting the meeting

- The date, hour, and location of the meeting

- The list of those present and those absent

- A reading of previous minutes and their approval or amendment

- Unfinished business

- New business

- The date of the next meeting

- The time of adjournment

- The signature of the recorder

Corporate Minutes

All corporations must document the minutes of shareholder and board of directors meetings.

In many states, the absence of proper meeting minutes may be a liability for the corporation, especially when the shareholders are also on the board of directors or there are close relationships among board members.

All corporations in the United States are required to hold annual shareholder's meetings to elect directors. The bylaws of most corporations require the board of directors to have annual meetings.

At corporate meetings the following actions will normally be approved by the board of directors:

- Election of officers of the corporation

- New business policies and plans

- Creation of committees and assignments

- Issuing and selling stock

- Approval of the sale, transfer, lease, or exchange of any corporate property or assets

- Approval of mergers and reorganizations

- Adoption of a pension, profit-sharing, or other employee benefit plans and stock option plans

- Approval of corporate borrowing and loans

- Entry into joint ventures

- Designation of corporate bank accounts and authorized signatures

- Changing an officer's compensation

- Entry into major contractual agreements

Corporate Resolutions

Formal resolutions may be made in one of these forms:

- WHEREAS it is necessary to . . . ; and

- WHEREAS conditions are such that . . . ; and

- Therefore be it

- RESOLVED, That . . . ; and be it

- RESOLVED further, That . . .

Note that the word *whereas* is in caps with no comma following it; the first word after it is not capitalized unless it is a proper name.

The word *resolved* is also set in caps but is followed by a comma and a capital letter.

Figure 39 Meeting Minutes

Minutes of Meeting of
the Historical Society of the University of Texas
Hotel Driscoll, Austin, Texas
May 1, 2012

At the meeting of the Historical Society of the University of Texas at Austin, some 100 charter members being present, the Society was called to order at 1:05 p.m. by Mr. John R. Combs, chairperson, who requested Mr. Warren T. Scaggs to serve as temporary secretary.

Mr. Combs dispensed with the reading of the minutes of the last meeting because a copy had been previously distributed to all members.

A communication from the National Historical Society, read and accepted by the Society, dealt with the planting of redbud trees throughout America.

A communication from Miss Harriet Allen of New York City asked that the Society refrain from its normal pattern of conducting spring tours throughout the State of Texas. Several members, after the reading, expressed disagreement with the views given by Miss Allen.

There was no unfinished business.

New business was the election of officers for the remaining current year. The following nominations were announced by Mr. Warren T. Scaggs, chairperson of the Nominating Committee:

President	Mrs. Rutherford Tinsdale
Secretary	Mr. Joseph Mapes
Treasurer	Mrs. Theodore R. Tollivar
Members of the Council	Ms. Louise Allen
	Mrs. Philip W. Crossman
	Mr. John Stobaugh
	Mrs. John C. McCann

After an unanswered call for nominations from the floor, it was moved by Mrs. William R. Metcalfe that the secretary cast one ballot for officers nominated. The motion was seconded and carried, and the officers were declared elected.

The next meeting of the Historical Society of the University of Texas at Austin will be held on June 11 at the Hotel Driscoll in Austin, Texas, at 1:00 p.m.

After congratulations to the newly elected officers by the chairperson, the Society adjourned at 3:25 p.m.

Warren T. Scaggs
Temporary Secretary

MEMORANDUM

An office **memorandum** or memo is often used to communicate with the employees of a company (Figure 40).

Most memos are sent using email; however, some types of communication are not appropriate for email and should instead be printed on paper and distributed.

Example: Confidential information or information that should not be forwarded

Memos that are directed to individuals should be printed and signed. If copies are sent to other parties, a notation to that effect should be made at the lower left corner of the form.

If a memo is confidential, it should be printed and enclosed in an envelope.

Figure 40 Memo

TO: Mary Anne Scott, Shipping Department Manager

FROM: Bob Brueck, President

DATE: May 12, 2014

SUBJECT: Meeting to discuss various overseas carriers

A meeting has been scheduled for Tuesday, May 12, in my office to discuss with several carrier representatives suggested methods and costs to deliver our products to international markets. Your attendance is requested.

Distribution:
Tom Alberton
Martha Reeves

MISSION STATEMENTS

A **mission statement** explains an organization's purpose, function, and reason for existing. A mission statement motivates employees, customers, and stockholders.

A mission statement guides decision making throughout the organization. Mission statements are often included in annual reports, company brochures, and Web sites, and they may also be printed and framed.

When writing a mission statement, consider the following tips (Figure 41):

- Include a statement of purpose.
- Include a description of the organization's business or principal activities.
- Include acknowledgment of all stakeholders.
- Optionally include the organization's goals and how they can be measured.

- Optionally include the organization's values and establish a sense of identity.

When brainstorming and writing a mission statement, ask and answer the following questions:

- Why was the organization created?

- Who are the stakeholders?

- What services does the organization provide?

- What identity do you want to project for the organization's products or services?

- What do you want to communicate to the community?

- What does the future look like for the organization?

- What organizational values are needed to achieve?

Figure 41 Mission Statement

PROJECT BLOOM MISSION STATEMENT

To promote the recognition, appreciation, and development of the human resources team through direct involvement, exciting communications, and sharing of innovative ideas, which result in the fullest appreciation of the diversity of the team.

NEWSLETTERS

Corporate **newsletters** are written to publicize news about a company or department for reading by employees or customers. Newsletters can be distributed on paper, sent via email, or posted on a Web site (Figure 42).

Regardless of whether they are paper or electronic, corporate newsletters usually involve a front page, inside articles, and announcements on the back page.

- Front page news focuses on achievements, success stories, or changes that affect the audience.

Example: a new contract, completion of a project, opening of a new office, launch of a new product, hiring of a new executive

---

- Inside articles:
    - Usually include departmental news that lets readers know what various parts of the company are doing.
    - Focus on departmental achievements and information about specific projects.
    - Often introduce newly hired employees to the rest of the company.
    - Can also highlight personal achievements of individual employees.
- Company updates are often included to communicate information about policies and procedures, make announcements about new equipment, and tell about training opportunities.
- Employee news articles often highlight employment anniversaries with the company.
- Calendar items list company-wide events, such as parties, quarterly or annual meetings, and training events.
- Employee announcements may list job openings, transfers, promotions, and other similar events.
- Filler material is used when space is available, including art, cartoons, or humorous items.

Newsletter content depends on whether the audience consists of the entire company, a single department, and whether customers will see it. Some companies publish newsletters that are distributed exclusively to customers, usually via email.

Newsletters for a customer audience should include:

- Information about new products and services
- Helpful tips of interest to customers
- Calendar items of importance to customers
- Information about major promotions involving employees who work directly with customers

Newsletters are more visually appealing if they include photographs.

Figure 42 Newsletter

GSA Office of Citizen Services and Communications

Intergovernmental Solutions Newsletter
Transparency and Open Government

Spring 2009

Transparency in Government

By Darlene Meskell
Director, Intergovernmental Solutions
GSA Office of Citizen Services and Communications

Newly elected President Barack Obama has taken bold steps to inaugurate an era of government openness and transparency. In one of his first official acts, the President issued a *Memorandum on Transparency and Open Government*, affirming his commitment to achieving an "unprecedented level of openness in government." Making known his belief that transparency is a fundamental responsibility of a democratic government, he called for the creation of an Open Government Directive that would require agencies to reveal their inner workings and make their data public.

A commitment to government accountability is at the heart of this message. By allowing citizens to "see through" its workings and investigate whether or not their leaders and organizations have met their expectations, the government brings the public into its inner circles and empowers citizens to contribute to decision-making. As citizens gain knowledge and understanding, their trust in government begins to grow.

Providing government data to citizens in a meaningful way will require a culture change, away from one where data are stored away for internal purposes to one that looks broadly at how data can be made accessible for re-use by the public. The federal website *Recovery.gov Reveals Details of the Stimulus Spending* on the $787 billion American Recovery and Reinvestment Act. It will put the data out in useable form so that people can slice, dice and mash it up to gain meaningful information about how government is working.

These data feeds create opportunities to look at government programs in new ways that could never have been imagined by the data collectors. The District of Columbia's *Apps for Democracy* Contest drew upon the public's imagination to make D.C. data more useful to constituents. Under the leadership of then-CTO Vivek Kundra, the District sponsored a contest seeking creative applications that use D.C. government data. The results were astonishing. The 47 entries submitted to *Apps for Democracy* within only 30 days "produced more savings for the D.C. government than any other initiative," according to Kundra, who has since been named federal CIO.

Continued on next page...

The Intergovernmental Solutions Newsletter is produced twice a year by the Intergovernmental Solutions Division, GSA Office of Citizens Services and Communications; Lisa Nelson, Editor. Send comments and suggestions to: lisa.nelson@gsa.gov.

(Courtesy of the U.S. General Services Administration)

Newsletter Articles

Consider the following guidelines when writing a newsletter article (Figure 43):

- Develop a title for the article that will accurately convey the topic or theme.
- Use a title that arouses curiosity.
- Use photographs that illustrate the story.
- Optionally, write an opening story summary that can be set apart in bold and included at the beginning of the article or in a sidebar.
- The lead sentence should introduce the topic, engage the reader, and focus on the reader's point of view.
- The body of the article should include relevant background and history, explain the implications of the topic, provide specific examples, and make suggestions.
  - Use transitions to connect the main points of the article.
- The article's conclusion should repeat the most important point and emphasize why it is important to the readers.
- Use appropriate language for the audience.
  - Avoid using jargon and clichés.
  - Avoid complicated sentence constructions and wordiness.
  - Keep paragraphs short and focused.
  - Use quotes and testimonials when appropriate.

Figure 43 Newsletter Article

WHAT DO YOU HAVE TO LOSE?

Have you noticed something missing from the 11th floor? Like 91 pounds?

That's how much the participants of the "What Do You Have to Lose" challenge lost all together. We had three teams of five people, and the team that had the highest percentage of weight loss at the end of the challenge won. The challenge kicked off on July 10 and wrapped up on September 7. In addition to losing 91 pounds, some participants brought their blood pressure down to a healthier level, others started an exercise program, and some replaced their daily cokes and coffees with 64 ounces of water.

Congratulations to the winners, The Fabulous Five (Donna Gilbert, Ken Willingham, Sterling Mabry, Cathy Price, and Darlene Warren). Together they had a 21% weight loss. The winners each received a $110 Visa Gift Card.

NOTICES

Notices highlight information that readers must understand to avoid mistakes, injuries, or damage to equipment. Notices are often included in user and training manuals.

The most common types of notices are:

- Notes—to serve as reminders or to avoid problems or mistakes (Figure 44)

- Tips—to provide useful troubleshooting or time-saving information (Figure 45).

- Warnings—about things that can cause major problems or an injury (Figure 46)

- Cautions—about things that can result in damage to equipment or data loss (Figure 47)

- Danger—about the possibility of serious or fatal injuries (Figure 48)

Notices should not only provide warnings, they should also explain the consequences for failure to abide by the advice offered in the notice.

Notices are formatted differently from the rest of the text in a document. They are placed within the text when needed. Caution and danger notices are placed before the content to which they apply. Special icons are sometimes used to emphasize a notice.

Notes are usually set apart in their own paragraph with the word *Note* in bold followed by a colon.

- Skip a line above and below the note and single space the note.

- Additional lines in the note should align with the word *Note*.

Figure 44 Note

COBRA Overage

A COBRA overage process was put in place to keep the benefits plan in compliance with IRS guidelines. When COBRA overage processing runs on Sunday and Wednesday night, it evaluates all employees' benefits and their covered dependents.

When a dependent reaches his or her 23rd birthday (without the disabled indicator checked), the system **automatically** drops the dependent from any medical and/or dental coverage.

Note: Home Office changes the disabled indicator in the database once an dependent is approved per plan guidelines.

Tips should be formatted like notes with the word *Tip* in bold and followed by a colon.

Figure 45 Tip

With the exceptions of the employee's retirement or eligibility for long-term disability (LTD), domestic partners are not eligible for COBRA independently of the employee. Events where COBRA should not be offered to a domestic partner include termination of the domestic partner relationship and death of the employee. The domestic partner coverage is terminated due to the employee's retirement or eligibility for the LTD health care plan, at which time the domestic partner will be given the option to elect COBRA continuation for a period of 18 months.

Tip: If an employee terminates and has domestic partner coverage under domestic partner medical, dental, or vision, the COBRA forms generated do not include COBRA rates for the domestic partner. To ensure that the employee is offered COBRA for the domestic partner, write the domestic partner's name, Social Security Number and date of birth on the COBRA form in the "Eligible Participants" section.

Warning notices should be formatted with the word *Warning* written in italics with approximately a half-inch of tab space separating the word from the message.

■ The text of the message should use the regular body font with no italics or bold.

■ Skip one line before and after the warning.

Figure 46 Warning Notice

The battery is one of the most important components on a vehicle today. It supplies not only the cranking amperage to start the engine, but also the initial voltage needed to run the onboard computer, ignition system, fuel injectors, lights, and all the vehicle accessories. Most of these systems require a minimum level of power to operate correctly. Having a good battery is absolutely essential for reliable vehicle starting and operation.

Warning: Be careful when handling batteries due to corrosive battery acid that may leak from the battery and damage your skin or eyes. Always wear gloves and eye protection.

Caution notices are formatted with the word *Caution* in bold and followed by a colon.

■ Caution should appear on a line by itself.

■ Skip one line before and after the caution notice.

■ The text for the message is single-spaced and is aligned with the word *Caution*.

Figure 47 Caution Notice

Multimedia is commonly defined as combining multiple forms of media such as audio, graphics, text, and video. Together, we will explore the multimedia control panel on your computer and find out how you can customize the features to enhance classroom presentations.

Caution:
Although we feel that it is important to show you how to control your settings, we recommend that you not make any changes to the system at this time. This is a multimedia course. It could be affected by any changes you make.

Danger notices should be formatted with the word *DANGER* in all caps, bold, and followed by a colon.

- Align the word *DANGER* with the normal text in the document.
- The rest of the text should be indented and aligned approximately 10 spaces from the left margin.
- Add a graphic box around the notice.

Figure 48 Danger Notice

It is a simple process to change wall switches around your home. You'll need a screwdriver, a replacement switch kit, a neon tester, and electrical tape.

> **DANGER:** Always shut off the power before beginning any electrical repair. Trip the breaker for the circuit that you will be working on. Use a neon tester on the outlet to be sure the power is off. If there is any doubt, trip the main breaker or remove the fuse and shut off power to entire house. Failure to follow these safety precautions may result in serious electrical shock, injury, or death.

PERMISSION LETTER

A **permission letter** is written to grant authority to someone for a specific purpose. Approval letters and authorization letters are similar.

When writing a permission letter, consider the following tips (Figures 49 and 50):

- Begin the letter by stating what permission is being granted and to whom it is being given.
- State the reasons for granting permission.
- Indicate the next steps the person is authorized to take.
- State any dates when the permission is effective, date of a specific event, and date the permission will expire.
- Include any other specific information regarding use of the permission.
- Include any special stipulations or guidelines that are required.
  - Outline any responsibilities.

Permission letters are typically written to:

- Approve a request.
- Approve a vacation or leave of absence.
- Approve the use of facilities.
- Give permission to be photographed as a model.
- Approve the use of a company vehicle.
- Authorize the use of copyrighted material.
- Grant permission to attend a conference or training session.
- Authorize medical treatment.
- Authorize work on a project.
- Delegate authority.
- Delegate a special project.
- Authorize research.

(text continues on page 98)

Figure 49 Permission Letter Granting Permission

PHOTO IMAGE GRANT OF RIGHTS AND RELEASE

In consideration of the opportunity to have my image published and other good and valuable consideration, the receipt and sufficiency of which is hereby acknowledged, the undersigned ("Releasor") hereby grants XYZ Corporation, its affiliates and their permittees (collectively, "Releasees") the following rights with respect to the use of the Releasor's image in the photographs taken on August 25, 2012 described as follows: XYZ Training Photos.

1. To alter and edit Releasor's image without limitation.

2. To use and publish Releasor's image and, in conjunction with it, Releasor's name and biographical information, in any medium, whether now or hereafter existing, including without limitation, any online service or Web site, and for any purpose, including, without limitation, promotional, advertising and marketing purposes.

With regard to these rights, Releasor releases and discharges Releasees and each of them from any and all claims and demands arising out of or in connection with the use of such photograph(s), the images therein (whether altered or unaltered) and Releasor's name and biographical information, including, without limitation, any claim for defamation, misappropriation, right of publicity, false light, invasion of privacy and copyright infringement.

The Photo Image Grant of Rights and Release constitutes an Agreement between Releasor and XYZ Corporation and contains the entire understanding between the parties. It cannot be modified except by written agreement signed by both parties and shall be governed and construed in accordance with the laws of the State of Georgia.

_____   _____

By: Signature   Date

_____

Name

_____

Address

_____

Figure 50 Permission Letter Requesting Permission

March 21, 2012

Communication Enterprises
3211 West Peachtree Street
Dunwoody, GA 32311

Dylan Wilson
Atlanta Community College
1311 West Northfield Drive
Decatur, GA 30133

Dear Mr. Wilson:

This letter confirms our recent telephone conversation regarding the use of a transcript of your Communications 101 course lecture on media responsibility in the June issue of our corporate newsletter.

I am responsible for editing the newsletter, and recently I heard you speak at a Technical Communications Association meeting on this subject. After speaking with you, I now know this talk is part of your regular course lectures at Atlanta Community College.

Our corporate newsletter is distributed to approximately 30,000 employees. It is an internal-only publication.

Please indicate your approval of this permission by signing this letter where indicated below and returning it to me as soon as possible. I have enclosed a self-addressed stamped envelope for that purpose.

Thank you very much for agreeing to let us publish your lecture.

Sincerely,

Al Gordon

Al Gordon
Communications Manager

Permission granted for the use requested above

_____   _____
Dylan Wilson   Date

POLICIES, RULES, OR GUIDELINES

Policies are rules or guidelines for a specific business process. They are formal corporate-wide instructions that must be followed by everyone within the organization. Violation of policies may result in disciplinary action. New policies must be approved by corporate management. (Figure 51.)

Rules are less formal than policies and define acceptable behavior within a particular department or division.

■ Rules may not impact the entire organization.

■ New rules must be approved by department or division heads.

■ Violation of rules may result in disciplinary action.

Guidelines suggest ways of handling certain situations.

■ Violating a guideline does not necessarily involve sanctions.

■ A subject matter expert should approve guidelines.

Policies address a particular problem or issue and specific groups of employees.

■ Policies must be formally shared with the group of employees who will be governed by the language.

■ Employee handbooks are often published with company policies and distributed to all employees.

To write a policy, rule, or guideline, follow these steps:

■ Create an outline of the topics that could be covered by the policy, rule, or guideline.

■ State the purpose of the policy, rule, or guideline.

■ State clearly what the policy, rule, or guideline allows and doesn't allow.

■ Explain to whom the policy, rule, or guideline applies.

■ Provide any background information that provides context on why the policy, rule, or guideline is needed.

- List any legislation that governs the policy, rule, or guideline.

- Describe any specific procedure that must be followed.
  - Use short paragraphs or numbered steps.
  - Group tasks together under subheadings.

- Explain what to do if violations occur.

- Explain any terminology that may be confusing to a general audience of employees.

- List any special circumstances when the policy, rule, or guideline does not apply.

- List any time restraints if applicable, including the effective date.

Figure 51 Policy

WHO IS ENTITLED TO BENEFITS UNDER COBRA

There are three elements to qualifying for COBRA benefits. COBRA establishes specific criteria for plans, qualified beneficiaries, and qualifying events:

Qualified Beneficiaries—A qualified beneficiary generally is an individual covered by a group health plan on the day before a qualifying event who is either an employee, the employee's spouse, or an employee's dependent child. In certain cases, a retired employee, the retired employee's spouse, and the retired employee's dependent children may be qualified beneficiaries. In addition, any child born to or placed for adoption with a covered employee during the period of COBRA coverage is considered a qualified beneficiary. Agents, independent contractors, and directors who participate in the group health plan may also be qualified beneficiaries.

Qualifying Events—Qualifying events are certain events that would cause an individual to lose health coverage. The type of qualifying event will determine who the qualified beneficiaries are and the amount of time that the plan must offer the health coverage to them under COBRA.

(continues)

Figure 51 *(continued)*

Qualifying Events for Employees:

■ Voluntary or involuntary termination of employment for reasons other than gross misconduct

■ Reduction in the number of hours of employment

Qualifying Events for Spouses:

■ Voluntary or involuntary termination of the covered employee's employment for any reason other than gross misconduct

■ Reduction in the hours worked by the covered employee

■ Covered employee's becoming entitled to Medicare

■ Divorce or legal separation of the covered employee

■ Death of the covered employee

Qualifying Events for Dependent Children:

■ Loss of dependent child status under the plan rules

■ Voluntary or involuntary termination of the covered employee's employment for any reason other than gross misconduct

■ Reduction in the hours worked by the covered employee

■ Covered employee's becoming entitled to Medicare

■ Divorce or legal separation of the covered employee

■ Death of the covered employee

POWERPOINT PRESENTATIONS

PowerPoint presentations are created to provide visual aids during oral presentations, sales presentations, and as stand-alone computer-based training. (Figures 52–55.) When creating PowerPoint presentations, consider the following tips:

■ Slide designs should focus the audience's attention on a particular aspect of each slide.

- Don't use too much text.
- Use contrasting colors, different text sizes, bold, or italics to set apart a particular element on the screen.
  - Highlight individual lines of text that are the focus of the slide.
- Bulleted text lines should be aligned to give the page an elegant look.
  - Keep all bullets on the same level grammatically parallel.
  - Indent text from the bullet symbols by a consistent space for all levels of bullets.
  - Avoid big paragraphs of text that fill the slide.
    - Use bullets, headings, and subheadings instead.
- Repeat visual elements and text throughout the presentation to focus on key points and to unify the presentation.
  - Repeat headings from slide to slide when appropriate.
  - Repeat text from slide to slide, while highlighting a different line on each slide.
- Group similar items on the slide to show a relationship.
  - Use subheadings with nested bullets for a list.
  - Use a graphic with associated text to show a visual connection to the text.
- Use sans serif fonts like Helvetica, Swiss, Arial, Avant Garde, and Modern.
  - Avoid mixing serif and sans serif fonts within the same presentation.
- Apply background shading for presentations that will be projected.
  - Use a white background for presentations that will be printed and distributed on paper.
  - If shading is used, use a gradient that gradually changes from light to dark or from one color to another to add visual depth to the presentation.
  - Apply a consistent color scheme to the entire presentation.
    - Do not use differently colored backgrounds for each slide in the presentation.

- Create styles for the entire presentation using Slide Master to:
  - Set the text placement as well as font size and color on all slides.
  - Keep the presentation consistent.
- Use Notes Master to insert speaker notes into the presentation.
  - When printed on paper, the slide appears at the top of the page and the notes appear at the bottom.
- Use Handout Master to add text and artwork to audience handouts.
- To save time when designing a presentation, use PowerPoint templates that are prebuilt and professionally designed.
  - Templates are available within the PowerPoint application.
  - Additional templates can be downloaded from the Internet.
- Use charts, photos, or illustrations that communicate visually.
  - Free clipart is available within PowerPoint.
  - Bar charts and pie charts can be created in PowerPoint.
    - Organizational charts can also be created within PowerPoint.
  - The Smart Art Graphics feature, available within the PowerPoint program, allows you to insert nice looking diagrams.
  - Digital cameras can be used to take photographs that can be imported into PowerPoint and placed on a slide.
  - AutoShapes allows you to create geometric shapes, arrows, and lines to help illustrate your slides.
- Videos, animation, and sound can be added to slides to create a multimedia presentation.

Planning a Presentation

Consider the following guidelines as you plan your presentation.

- Determine your goal and objectives.

Example: Do you want to persuade or inform?

- Keep the presentation simple and focused.

    - A clear message with more impact is more likely to achieve results than an unfocused one.

    - A complicated message is muddled and will leave the audience confused and frustrated.

    - Keep the number of topics covered to a minimum.

- Design the presentation like creating a story.

    - Organize the content with a beginning, middle, and end.

- Design for drama.

    - Pique your audience's interest toward the end of the presentation and deliver the central conclusion of your message when you have the full attention of everyone.

- Plan your media selection.

    - Will you use slides and a digital projector, printed handouts, or both?

- Think and plan ahead.

    - If you give the audience handouts before the show, they can follow along and write notes directly on the handouts.

    - Handouts also give the audience something to reference if they have trouble seeing the screen.

    - If you distribute handouts at the end of the presentation, you can avoid giving away any planned surprises.

- Consider the subject matter.

    - The tone of your presentation depends on the type of presentation: training seminar, presentation to managers or employees, or a sales presentation to customers.

- Consider the audience's:

    - Familiarity with the subject matter

    - Composition (will the audience be exclusively employees, or customers, or mixed?)

    - Size (large audiences dictate the need for more structure and formality; small audiences may be less formal, giving you more room for improvisation and one-on-one interaction)

■   Consider the environment for the presentation.

    ■   How visible is the screen from each part of the room?

    ■   If visibility is in question, include handouts with printed versions of each slide.

    ■   If you are not familiar with the equipment, arrange time for setting up and rehearsing your presentation before delivering the real thing.

■   Practice delivering your presentation.

    ■   Deliver your presentation to a coworker or friend and ask for a critique.

Figure 52 Slide with Bulleted Lists,
a Graphical Background, and Photo

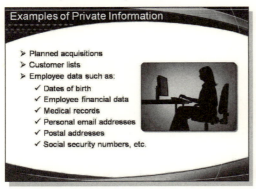

Figure 53 Slide with Title,
Bulleted Subtitle, and Pie Chart

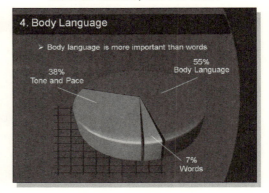

Figure 54 Slide with
PowerPoint WordArt

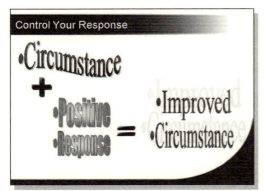

Figure 55 Slide with
Graphics Rather Than Text

PRESS RELEASES

A **press release** is a written communication directed at the news media for the purpose of making an announcement. When writing a press release, consider the following guidelines (Figure 56):

■ Lay out your document on an 8½ x 11-inch page.

■ Provide wide margins and double-space the copy.

■ Include a release date at the top of the page.

■ Provide a contact name and address. Provide as much contact information as possible, including fax, email, and Web site addresses.

■ Include the phrase "For Immediate Release" along with a contact name and phone number. If the release date is in the future, instead say, "For Release on [date]."

■ Include a suggested headline.

■ Start your first paragraph with the location in all caps, followed by the month and day.

■ Summarize your story in the first paragraph, including who, what, why, where, when, and how.

■ Make sure the first 10 words are effective; they are the most important.

■ Elaborate on the details, including quotes from important sources.

■ Make sure the information is newsworthy by suggesting other tie-ins. Pick an angle. Try to make your press release timely by tying it to current events or social issues.

■ Avoid excessive use of adjectives and fancy language. Use only enough words to tell your story.

■ Use the active, not passive, voice. Verbs in the active voice bring your press release to life.

■ Avoid jargon specific to your organization that might not be recognized by other readers.

■ Answer the question, why should anyone care?

■ Use real-life examples, if possible, that include stories of the people involved.

- Raise other questions or suggest topics of interest, if you are trying to generate a feature story or radio or TV interview.
- Suggest in a covering pitch letter an interview with the principal person or organization involved, such as the company CEO or a book author.
- Type the word *more* at the end of each page.
- At the end of your release, type ### and center it.

Figure 56 Press Release

October 1, 2014

Contact Name
Address
City, State, Zip
Email
Web Address

For Immediate Release
Contact: Jason Brown—770-555-1234

BRONSON MEDIA SIGNS $8 MILLION CONTRACT WITH VIDEOLOGIES, INC. TO BE EXCLUSIVE PROVIDER OF CIRCULATION SYSTEMS, NETWORK, AND APPLICATIONS.

ATLANTA, Oct 1—Bronson Media, the largest American newspaper owner, signed an $8 million contract making Videologies, Inc. the exclusive provider of circulation systems, network and applications for print media holdings.

Videologies will now provide circulation software for all of Bronson Media's newspapers, including the *Los Angeles Herald, The Seattle Constitution,* and *the Atlanta Daily.* The contract was awarded to Videologies after an extensive product and company review. Bronson Media will take advantage of the entire line of Videologies circulation software. VID 4.2 is a program specially designed for print media to chart production and material costs to optimize productivity. VID Router allows newspapers to make routing decisions and design delivery routes based on scanned maps.

Mark Giddings, vice president of print media operations at Bronson Media, commented, "The contract with Videologies is a big step forward for Bronson's newspapers. It will allow us to standardize circulation and production systems, making cooperation between our print media holdings more efficient and effective."

###

PROCEDURES

Procedures are instructions that explain how to perform a particular task (Figure 57).

To write a procedure:

- State the goal of the procedure.

   Example: This procedure tells you how to install a cable modem.

- The heading for the procedure may also state the goal.

   Example: Installing a Cable Modem

- If specific supplies or knowledge are needed for the procedure, provide a list before detailing the steps.

   Example: Before you start, you'll need the following: coaxial cable, pliers, and a screwdriver.

- If a certain level of experience is necessary, provide a list for whom the procedures are intended.

   Example: Before attempting this procedure, you should have a basic understanding of an operating system.

- When is it necessary to use specific terminology to describe the procedure, use only what is absolutely necessary.
    - Don't overload the procedure with unnecessary jargon.
    - Explain any specialized technical terms that are used.
- Provide an estimate of how long it will take to complete the procedure.
- List the steps in the procedure using numbered lists.
- Break the steps in the overall procedure into smaller sections.
    - Limit the number of steps to 10 in each section.
    - Each section should have its own title.
- If a particular step has substeps, indent a secondary list using letters to designate them.
- Describe only one step at a time.
    - Each step should describe one task.
- Include illustrations where appropriate.
- If certain conditions apply or if performing a step will cause something to happen, present this information at the beginning of the step.

Example: To shut down the computer, click the **Start** button, then click **Turn Off the Computer**.

- When someone else is supposed to perform a particular step in the procedure, describe who is responsible and what he or she will do.

Example: The licensing department will accept your serial number, and will email you an activation code.

- At the end of the procedure, include a statement that tells users that the procedure is complete and what the result is likely to be.

Example: That completes the steps for installing the cable modem. The power and Internet lights should be solid green.

- Provide references to other useful information.

Figure 57 Procedures

WALKTHROUGH—PASTE SPECIAL > VALUES

In this walkthrough, you will use the Paste Special > Values function to convert the result of a formula to text.

1. Continue with the TTFFP—Daily Activity Exercise.xls file, which should already be open.

2. Select cell **I2**, the cell your concatenating formula is in.

3. Select **Edit > Copy**.

4. Select **Edit > Paste Special**.

5. Select the **Values** radio button.

6. Click **OK**.

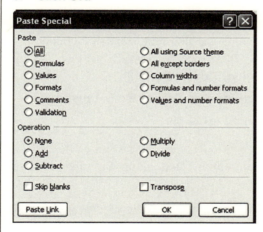

Note how your formula has been transformed into text.

7. Save your work by clicking **File > Save As**, and then changing the name of the file to **"Daily Activity Exercise A"** and then click the **Save** button.

8. Close the spreadsheet by clicking **File > Close**.

That completes this walkthrough.

PROGRESS REPORTS

Progress reports are written to inform a supervisor about the status of a project. These reports detail what was completed for the previous period, what percentage of the work has been completed, and what is planned for the next period. Any problems or issues are listed in the report.

Progress reports let management know about the overall health of a project and its team members. Progress reports also let everyone on the team know how the overall project is going.

These reports range from simple memos for small projects, to informal letters, to formal reports.

- Memos are often used for internal progress reports.
- Progress report letters are sent to outside clients.
- Formal progress reports are also sent to outside clients.

All progress reports include (Figure 58):

- What work has been completed since the last report
- What work is currently being performed
- What work is planned
- Individual tasks, sometimes listed, along with their completion percentages
- The progress of different stages of development and categories for different departments (may be listed for large projects)

Project reports prepared for outside customers may also include:

- The project purpose
- Objectives
- Scope or limitations
- Start date and completion date
- Current development phase
- Team members

(text continues on page 114)

Figure 58 Progress Report

ERP UPGRADE PROJECT STATUS REPORT

Name of Project: ERP Upgrade
Date: July 27, 2012
Project Manager: Mary Dawson
Sponsor: Allan Cummings

Project Objectives:

Upgrade the existing ERP application to position Acme Industries to maintain vendor support for the application and to consider undertaking projects, after the upgrade, which will implement new functionality offered in the ERP system.

Implementation Date: August 20, 2012
Current Phase: QA Testing/UAT Testing/Implementation Planning

Project Management Summary:

The upgrade project remains on track. 14 business days until we began our upgrade implementation!

ISSUE

Integrated QA test environment was planned for May 7 and is not completely ready.

Update—Stellent configuration issue was resolved and testing for Stellent will start next week.

QA Testing—The formal QA testing period is over; however, QA testing will continue for some items, including:

- HR/benefits—75% complete. Outstanding are items associated with HCFA, MSY, Retirees, and FSA.

- eApps—95% complete. Outstanding are items associated with integration testing that we delayed/not operating in our integrated test environment.

- Security—90% complete. Outstanding items are 4 reports that have been on hold pending resolution to reporting problems in QA. Testing planned for next week is in development.

System testing and UAT have been combined for HRM, HRM Data Prep, Hyperion, and Stellent. Status for these will be reported under user acceptance testing.

(continues)

Figure 58 *(continued)*

Third-party interface testing is in process. The team resolved outstanding issues with the integrated testing environment.

User Acceptance Testing—Continued formal UAT sessions. UAT testing is expected to be complete on August 3.

- HR/Benefits—50% complete—sessions scheduled through 8/3
- Payroll—85% complete—sessions scheduled through 7/27; interface testing will run into next week
- Authoria—80% complete—sessions scheduled through 7/30
- 401(k)—60% complete—sessions scheduled through 8/3
- Compensation—90% complete—sessions scheduled through 7/27
- HRM—90% complete—sessions scheduled through 8/3. Outstanding issue with home phone
- HRM Data Prep—50% complete—sessions scheduled through 8/3
- eApps—0% complete—session scheduled for 7/30
- Security—90% complete; retest sessions scheduled for early next week
- eRecruit—50% complete; sessions scheduled through 7/31
- Hyperion/EDW—70% complete; sessions scheduled through 7/30
- Stellent—0% complete; sessions scheduled though 8/3
- Pension—UAT is complete
- ESPP—UAT is complete
- Simple Steps—UAT is complete
- PDR—UAT is complete
- LMS—UAT is complete
- Total Comp—UAT is complete

Load Testing—Began load testing for eRecruit—expected completion is 7/31. Load testing for the eApps will follow with completion expected on 8/10.

Parallel Testing—Completed parallel #3 with excellent results. 34 of 36 sites have signed off as of 8 a.m. Friday.

Development: Development team is on track with issues and defects. Retrofitting for public and private queries continues. Continued refinement of implementation plan. Planned dress rehearsal—Test Move 7. Completed some pre-implementation tasks in PROD—copied software, set up data files, and added temporary space for backups.

eRecruit: Continued QA testing and UAT testing. Received signoff from subsidiaries. Additional sessions are scheduled for next week.

Training, documentation, and communication tasks are on schedule.

Deliverables completed last week:

Task	Complete Date	Comments
Milestone: Completed eRecruit system testing	7/23	No problems.
Milestone: PDR UAT complete	7/23	Report format issues were resolved.
Milestone: Simple Steps UAT complete	7/23	No problems.
Milestone: Total Compensation UAT complete	7/26	Data sync issue was resolved.

Deliverables scheduled for completion in next 2 weeks:

Task	Due Date	Comments
Milestone: eRecruit Query Development Complete	8/9	Mark Lester is out for medical leave.
Milestone: eRecruit Technical Process Flow Complete	8/13	
Milestone: Coordination of Division Portal links and URL changes for eRecruit complete	8/20	Outside focus group members are needed.

(continues)

Figure 58 *(continued)*

Resource Changes: None.

Future Meetings:

- Daily UAT testing sessions

- Daily Parallel testing sessions and morning meetings

- Full Team Status Meeting 7/31 ** Moved to Tuesday for this week only **

- Weekly Training, Documentation, and Communications Team Meeting 7/30

- Weekly Implementation Meeting 8/1

- Weekly IT Leads Team Meeting 8/1

- Weekly HR/Benefits Analyst Team Meeting 8/1

- Weekly QA Team Meeting 8/2

- Weekly Payroll Analyst Team Meeting 8/2

- Weekly Developers Team Meeting 8/2

PROPOSALS

Proposals usually consist of a bid and a description of a project, and they are sent to a customer. Many proposals are sent after a prospective customer makes a request for proposal (RFP).

There are several different types of proposals:

- Internal proposals written for someone within the same business

- External proposals written to another business or government agency

- Solicited proposals that are written and sent in response to and in accordance with the guidelines described in an RFP

- Unsolicited proposals that are sent to convince a potential customer to do business with you

Most proposals include the following sections (Figure 59):

- Cover letter—to be sent with a proposal

- Introduction—introducing the proposal, referring to previous contacts with the customer, and providing an overview of the contents of the proposal

- Background—information about the need for the project
- Benefits—describing how the proposed solution will solve the problems discussed in the background section
- Project description—describing what is involved in the project, including specifications for the end product
- Method—discussing how the project will be completed
- Schedule—detailing the project timeline
- Qualifications—discussing the organization's qualifications for completing the project
- Budget—listing the costs
- Conclusion—final words about why the submitter of the proposal should be awarded the project

When preparing a proposal, consider the following:

- Make sure you address everything asked for, if responding to an RFP.
- Identify all the tasks that are necessary to complete the project.
- Break out the budget into individual line items and include hourly rates if applicable.

(text continues on page 125)

Figure 59 Proposal for Video Production Services

LPS TRAINING
Video Production Proposal

Submitted to:

Andy Norvell

SAR Office Manager

BSP Energy Products Company

By:

Videologies

Acworth, Georga

(Courtesy of Videologies, Inc.)

(continues)

Figure 59 *(continued)*

INTRODUCTION

This proposal is for the production of an LPS training video for BSP Energy's SAR Department.

BSP Energy's request includes the following requirements:

- Limit video length to approximately 35 minutes
- Deliver the finished video by November 30, 2012
- Shoot at two sites in either New Jersey or Los Angeles basin area
- Create 10 minutes of material on drilling, monitor well installation, and sampling tasks
- Create 10 minutes of material on trenching, and SVE installation LPOs
- Create 6 minutes of material for supervisor feedback sessions
- Create 9 minutes of material featuring a host on camera for introductions and other commentary

After careful examination of these requirements, Videologies proposes the following:

- Research and scriptwriting with access to subject matter experts in the Atlanta area or via telephone or email
- Pre-production location visit by our producer
- Five days of production at two different locations in either New Jersey or Los Angeles
- One day of production in the Atlanta area for shooting an on-camera host
- Video still graphics to illustrate concepts
- Text and graphics
- Optional CD-ROM version
- Optional Streaming Video version for Web distribution

SPECIFICATIONS

The LPS Training video produced for BSP Energy will include the following specifications:

- 35-minute video script

- Producer services to coordinate all aspects of the production

- Video production using XDCAM HD format

- Video production crew including a director, camera operator, and lighting assistants as appropriate

- Use of a professional actor or actress for on-camera and voice-over narration

- One pre-production trip to either New Jersey or Los Angeles to scout locations and coordinate activities

- One five-day trip to either New Jersey or Los Angeles for shooting segments A, B, and C as outlined in the LPS Training Video Work Scope provided by Andy Nowell of BSP Energy

- Nonlinear post production to edit a master tape for duplication

- Video graphics for illustrating concepts

- Titles and transitional effects

- Background music

- Two approval copies

- One Blu-Ray DVD master for duplication

BSP Energy will provide the following logistical and review requirements:

- Script review and approval

- Locations

- All necessary props

- Personnel for demonstrations and activities described in the script

- Subject matter experts

- Company logos

(continues)

Figure 59 *(continued)*

TREATMENT

Based on our June 18, 2012 meeting, we propose a video treatment that utilizes an on-camera host to guide us through the video.

The host will be shot on location in the Atlanta area and will be used to introduce the content on camera and then narrate sequences shot on location.

Since the purpose of the video is to give viewers practice in observing LPO situations, we will divide the video into short two- to three-minute segments. Students will choose segments from a menu. Each segment will have a title screen describing its content. The on-camera host will introduce each segment and explain what viewers are about to see. Instructions will be given for viewers to practice their LPO observations as they watch scenes of various work practices. The narrator will describe the scene but will allow viewers to make and record their own observations. Following this sequence, we will replay the same sequence again, this time with the narrator pointing out all the possible observations. This will allow the viewers to check their answers.

Because students will watch these sequences twice, once with overview narration, and once again with the narrator describing the LPO observations, the finished video will be longer than 35 minutes. However, for purposes of budgeting, we are planning on no more than 35 minutes of original material. Repeating material in the same video will not increase the budget.

It is understood that only a sampling of possible LPO observations that may occur in an activity such as drilling will be featured in the video. We will work with BSP Energy's subject matter experts to construct scenes that feature as many work practice observations (both good and bad) as possible.

The training will be designed so that it can be self-paced. As part of our deliverables to BSP Energy, we will produce a short student guide (in Adobe Acrobat PDF format) that provides instructions for each video segment activity. We assume that BSP Energy will provide copies of LPO forms, so students can fill out the forms while watching the video.

The following LPO target areas will be featured in the video:

- Drilling, monitor well installation, and sampling tasks
- Trenching and SVE installation LPOs
- Supervisor feedback sessions

PRODUCTION

The production process will consist of the following stages:

- Content analysis and design

- Scriptwriting

- Video production

- Graphics production

- Post production

- Programming

- Study guide production

- Revisions

- Final mastering

Content Analysis and Design

Videologies will meet with subject matter experts and review previously produced materials, such as LPO forms and LPS handbooks. We will work together to plan our work practice scenarios to feature specific LPO opportunities for students. After completing content analysis, Videologies will create a design document that summarizes our plans for the video.

Scriptwriting

After a design is approved by BSP Energy, the scriptwriter will draft a script in a two-column format describing visuals and narration or suggested on-camera audio. This script will be submitted to BSP Energy for review. After this review, any revisions required will be made and a final script will be submitted for approval.

Video Production

After the script is approved, video production will begin. Video production will consist of the following:

- Five days of production on location at two sites in either New Jersey or Los Angeles

- One day of production in Atlanta to shoot the on-camera host

- Narration recording

(continues)

Figure 59 *(continued)*

Graphics Production

Video graphics will be created to illustrate concepts where appropriate. Title screens will also be created and added where appropriate.

Post Production

During post production, we will edit the raw footage, mix the audio, add music, insert graphics, and incorporate transitional effects where appropriate.

Study Guide Production

A short 10–20 page study guide will be created to facilitate the learning experience for self-paced training.

Final Mastering

After final approval of the video, a Blu-Ray DVD master will be delivered for duplication purposes.

OPTIONS

BSP Energy has requested that Videologies provide quotes on future upgrades of the video to CD-ROM and possible Web site delivery. In addition, we can provide VHS duplications upon request.

CD-ROM

The content created for the LPS Training video and study guide can be upgraded for delivery via CD-ROM. Depending on the design and content requirements, we can create a wide variety of CD-ROM–based programs ranging from a simple AVI video player to a more complex system incorporating additional audio instruction, graphics, simulations, and test questions.

The finished video segments can be converted to a Windows AVI video format at a screen size of 320×240 and played on a IBM PC compatible equipped with a CD-ROM drive, soundcard and speakers or headphones. We would recommend a minimum configuration of Pentium II 350 with an 8X CD-ROM drive.

As the least expensive option, we can create a CD that includes an autorun feature so installation is not necessary. Upon inserting the CD, the user will see a 640×480 menu screen that gives students access to a downloadable study guide, downloadable LPO forms, and menu choices for viewing the various video sequences (or lessons).

A more expensive alternative can include quiz and test questions, graphic and text screens, audio, and simulations for a more substantial learning experience. The course would require the use of a Web browser such as Internet Explorer to view content pages, access LPO forms, and view video and audio sequences. Test questions will provide feedback and remediation to ensure and document a student's comprehension.

Web Delivery

Videologies can provide streaming media versions of the finished video sequences in either Windows Media or Real Media formats compressed for playback at 300K speeds. Anything less than 300K compression produces quality that is too reduced for effective training. At least a 300K connection is required to view the files. This speed of connection is usually available with DSL, Cable Modem, or office LAN connections.

BSP Energy will need to provide a streaming media server (by purchasing a streaming media license from either Real Networks or Microsoft) in order to "stream" the videos. Without this server, the users must download each video sequence before playing it.

Videologies can provide services ranging from just supplying the media files to BSP Energy for posting on their own Web site, to creating a complete Web-based course similar to the CD-ROM version, complete with menus, graphics, and testing.

DELIVERABLES

This proposal calls for the following deliverables from Videologies:

- Design document
- Script
- One 10–20–page study guide in PDF format
- Two approval DVD copies
- One Blu-Ray DVD master

Optional deliverables include:

- CD-ROM version
- Windows Media or Real Media Web files
- DVD duplications

(continues)

Figure 59 *(continued)*

LOGISTICS AND SCHEDULE

Videologies proposes the following schedule for the video:

Begin project	August 8, 2012
Content research	August 8–17, 2012
Content design delivered	August 21, 2012
Design approval from BSP Energy	August 28, 2012
Scriptwriting and revisions	August 28–September 18, 2012
Script approval from BSP Energy	September 25, 2012
Location shoot in either New Jersey or Los Angeles	October 1–5, 2012
Host shoot in Atlanta	October 8, 2012
Study guide production	October 8–26, 2012
Graphics production	October 8–26, 2012
Post production	November 5–19, 2012
Approval copy review	November 20, 2012
Revisions	November 26–28, 2012
Final master delivered	November 30, 2012

Any delay by BSP Energy in reviewing scripts, providing personnel, or locations, may delay delivery of the final video.

BUDGET

The services provided by Videologies will require the following development budget:

Production Category	Amount
Producer Services	$ 2,800
Design, Analysis, and Research	2,800
Scriptwriting	2,800
Production Equipment	4,200
Production Crew	16,000
Talent	1,500
Other Misc. Production Costs (crew meals, videotape)	1,350
Graphics	1,250
Post Production (editing, music, and master duplication)	8,270
Travel Costs (hotel, car, air, per diem)	5,880
10% Cost Contingency for overtime and Videologies overages	4,685
Total	$51,535

(continues)

Figure 59 *(continued)*

RATES AND MANPOWER

Rates are based on the following:

- Writing, producing, directing services, and production crew at $50 per hour or $500 per day per person.

- Video production equipment rentals at $700 per day, includes camera, tripod, lights, monitors, waveform, and grip equipment.

- Post production services at $125 per hour.

- Graphic services at $50 per hour.

- Computer programming services at $75 per hour.

- AVI and streaming media conversation at $40 per finished minute.

- Professional union actor at $1,500 per day.

Estimated manpower requirements include:

- Writer—14 days

- Producer—7 days

- Director—6 days plus 2 travel days

- Camera operator—6 days plus 2 travel days

- Lighting specialist—6 days plus 2 travel days

- Production assistant—6 days plus 2 travel days

- Editor—60 hours

- Graphic artist—25 hours

- Professional union actor—1 day

Estimated equipment rental days include:

- Camera package—6 days

- Nonlinear editor—60 hours

QUESTIONNAIRES AND SURVEYS

Questionnaires and surveys are used to gather data about customers and employees for use in decision making, marketing, and the development of new products and services. (Figure 60.)

Questionnaires can be distributed on paper or online. Online surveys are especially helpful because they can be emailed as links and the results can be automatically tabulated into a database or spreadsheet.

Using a questionnaire is a multistage process involving the design and development of the questions, determining the survey group, conducting the survey, and then interpreting the results.

Questionnaires are usually designed to gather qualitative or quantitative data.

- Qualitative surveys ask about opinions and ask respondents to rate the quality of a product or service.
- Quantitative surveys measure how many people do a particular thing, such as use a product or watch a particular television channel.

Questionnaires are often used instead of personal interviews because:

- They can be inexpensive to create and use.
- The privacy of the participants can be protected.
- When used with other data, such as sales trends, they can be useful as a confirmation tool.

Consider the following steps when creating a questionnaire:

- The first step in creating a questionnaire is to define the objectives.
    - The questions should focus on obtaining specific information.
        - To determine qualitative data about a product or service, you must break down the qualities into various aspects that can be isolated and measured.
    - The question order should have a logical flow.
- The second step in creating a questionnaire is to write the questions.
    - Write an introduction to the questionnaire that explains its purpose.

- Provide instructions on how to answer the questions.
    - Explain the rating scale if one is used.
- Include demographic questions to gather information about the respondents.
    - This information is helpful later when you are analyzing the results and comparing responses among different groups of people.
    - Common demographic questions, including age, sex, level of education, annual earnings, and so forth.
    - Demographic questions are normally asked at the beginning of the questionnaire.
- There are two general types of survey questions: multiple-choice or fill-in-the-blank.
    - Fill-in-the-blank questions are more time-consuming during the data analysis phase.
    - Multiple choice questions make it easier to tabulate the responses and calculate percentages.
    - Multiple-choice questions also make it easier to track opinions over time to see how the same questionnaire is answered by similar groups of people over a specific period.
- For multiple-choice questions involving a rating scale, it is best to have an even number of rating choices.
    - Having an odd number of choices leaves respondents with a middle neutral choice, which is often used by respondents who are bored.
    - Having an even number of choices eliminates the possibility of neutral answers.
- Multiple-choice questions should have clear, distinct answer choices.
    - "Very often," "Often," and "Sometimes" answer choices can be interpreted differently by different respondents.
    - "Every day," "2 to 5 times a week," and "Once a month" answer choices are easier to interpret.

■ Avoid leading questions that imply a biased answer.

Example: A rating scale with choices like: "Incredible," "Superb," "Excellent," "Great," "Good"

Incorrect: Is this the best software you've ever used?

■ Avoid adjectives and adverbs in your questions; they imply a biased answer.

■ Avoid embarrassing questions that deal with personal or private matters.

■ Avoid hypothetical questions; they are based on fantasy rather than fact.

■ Avoid using *not* in your questions; this word can lead to double negatives and already implies a negatively biased answer.

After you've written the questions for the survey, proofread and test the survey on a small sampling of respondents.

■ Review the questionnaire with the test audience and work together to resolve any problems.

■ Revise the survey after the pilot test.

■ Put a date on the questionnaire, so that you can keep track of versions.

Figure 60 Survey

U.S. DEPARTMENT OF COMMERCE
Economics and Statistics Administration
U.S. CENSUS BUREAU

United States Census 2010

This is the official form for all the people at this address.
It is quick and easy, and your answers are protected by law.

Use a blue or black pen.

Start here

The Census must count every person living in the United States on April 1, 2010.

Before you answer Question 1, count the people living in this house, apartment, or mobile home using our guidelines.

- Count all people, including babies, who live and sleep here most of the time.

The Census Bureau also conducts counts in institutions and other places, so:

- Do not count anyone living away either at college or in the Armed Forces.
- Do not count anyone in a nursing home, jail, prison, detention facility, etc., on April 1, 2010.
- Leave these people off your form, even if they will return to live here after they leave college, the nursing home, the military, jail, etc. Otherwise, they may be counted twice.

The Census must also include people without a permanent place to stay, so:

- If someone who has no permanent place to stay is staying here on April 1, 2010, count that person. Otherwise, he or she may be missed in the census.

1. How many people were living or staying in this house, apartment, or mobile home on April 1, 2010?

   Number of people =

2. Were there any additional people staying here April 1, 2010 that you did not include in Question 1?
   Mark X all that apply.

   ☐ Children, such as newborn babies or foster children
   ☐ Relatives, such as adult children, cousins, or in-laws
   ☐ Nonrelatives, such as roommates or live-in baby sitters
   ☐ People staying here temporarily
   ☐ No additional people

3. Is this house, apartment, or mobile home —
   Mark X ONE box.

   ☐ Owned by you or someone in this household with a mortgage or loan? Include home equity loans.
   ☐ Owned by you or someone in this household free and clear (without a mortgage or loan)?
   ☐ Rented?
   ☐ Occupied without payment of rent?

4. What is your telephone number? We may call if we don't understand an answer.
   Area Code + Number

OMB No. 0607-0919-C: Approval Expires 12/31/2011.

Form **D-61** (1-15-2009)

USCENSUSBUREAU

5. Please provide information for each person living here. Start with a person living here who owns or rents this house, apartment, or mobile home. If the owner or renter lives somewhere else, start with any adult living here. This will be Person 1.
   What is Person 1's name? Print name below.

   Last Name

   First Name   MI

6. What is Person 1's sex? Mark X ONE box.
   ☐ Male   ☐ Female

7. What is Person 1's age and what is Person 1's date of birth?
   Please report babies as age 0 when the child is less than 1 year old. Print numbers in boxes.

   Age on April 1, 2010   Month   Day   Year of birth

→ NOTE: Please answer BOTH Question 8 about Hispanic origin and Question 9 about race. For this census, Hispanic origins are not races.

8. Is Person 1 of Hispanic, Latino, or Spanish origin?

   ☐ No, not of Hispanic, Latino, or Spanish origin
   ☐ Yes, Mexican, Mexican Am., Chicano
   ☐ Yes, Puerto Rican
   ☐ Yes, Cuban
   ☐ Yes, another Hispanic, Latino, or Spanish origin — Print origin, for example, Argentinean, Colombian, Dominican, Nicaraguan, Salvadoran, Spaniard, and so on.

9. What is Person 1's race? Mark X one or more boxes.

   ☐ White
   ☐ Black, African Am., or Negro
   ☐ American Indian or Alaska Native — Print name of enrolled or principal tribe.

   ☐ Asian Indian   ☐ Japanese   ☐ Native Hawaiian
   ☐ Chinese   ☐ Korean   ☐ Guamanian or Chamorro
   ☐ Filipino   ☐ Vietnamese   ☐ Samoan
   ☐ Other Asian — Print race, for example, Hmong, Laotian, Thai, Pakistani, Cambodian, and so on.   ☐ Other Pacific Islander — Print race, for example, Fijian, Tongan, and so on.

   ☐ Some other race — Print race.

10. Does Person 1 sometimes live or stay somewhere else?
    ☐ No   ☐ Yes — Mark X all that apply.

    ☐ In college housing   ☐ For child custody
    ☐ In the military   ☐ In jail or prison
    ☐ At a seasonal   ☐ In a nursing home
      or second residence   ☐ For another reason

→ If more people were counted in Question 1, continue with Person 2.

(Courtesy of the U.S. Department of Commerce)

REFERENCE LETTERS

A **reference letter** states the qualifications for a person seeking employment. It offers an endorsement of the person's job performance, skills, and character. A reference letter may be accepted in lieu of contacting references on the phone.

A reference letter should include (Figure 61):

- How and for how long you know the person

- Your qualifications for writing the reference letter

- A list of the person's qualities and skills

- Key points about the person that the reader should note

- Examples that back up your opinions about the person

- Your contact information

Reference letters are typically written to:

- Recommend someone for a job.

- Recommend someone who has applied to school.

- Endorse a political candidate.

- Provide a credit reference.

- Recommend a service or product.

- Recommend someone for club membership.

Figure 61 Reference Letter

John Davidson
Videologies, Inc.
1313 Old Alabama Highway
Atlanta, GA 30121

Hello,

This is a letter of recommendation for Peter Carson.

Peter has worked with me for the past year in the role of training technology manager at Videologies, Inc., a multimedia and training development business.

At Videologies, Peter worked on designing a training course for our Learning Management System. He designed and created a webinar presentation and a student exercise workbook.

Peter also worked on three multiday instructor-led courses on the subject of accounting practices. Peter did analysis, created the design, coordinated with the customer, and created workbooks and PowerPoint presentations.

I highly recommend Peter Carson for instructional design and course development projects.

Sincerely,

John Davidson

John Davidson
Vice President

REFUSAL LETTER

A **refusal letter** is written to deny a request, decline an invitation, or reply negatively to a suggestion. When writing a refusal letter, consider the following tips (Figure 62):

- Be as diplomatic as possible to avoid hurt feelings.

- Open the letter with a sincere statement that explains that you are refusing the request.

- Explain your reasons for the refusal, and include any evidence to back up your decision.

- Offer alternatives to the readers that might have a better chance of being accepted.

- Be courteous and wish the reader success elsewhere.

Refusal letters are typically written to:

- Decline an invitation or appointment.

- Decline a claim request from a customer.

- Turn down a request for a donation.

- Decline a job offer, promotion, or transfer.

- Reject an application for employment.

- Decline to join an organization.

- Terminate a business relationship.

- Decline a request to write a letter of recommendation.

- Turn down a suggestion.

- Decline a request for credit.

- Decline a gift.

- Decline orders or requests for information.

Figure 62 Refusal Letter

February 21, 2012

Buffalo Graphics
3133 Highway 9
Roswell, GA 32311

Dylan Wilson
Atlanta Community College
1311 West Northfield Drive
Decatur, GA 30133

Dear Mr. Wilson:

Thank you for invitation to be a guest lecturer in your communications class at Atlanta Community College. I'm sorry, but I'll have to decline the invitation.

I recently became the president of the Atlanta Communications Association, and these added responsibilities have already required more time than I have available. I would suggest that you contact Al Gordon, the ex-president of ACA. He may be available and with his experience, he should make an excellent guest lecturer.

I am honored to have been invited by you. You are well respected within the communications industry, and I wish you all the best with your class.

Sincerely,

Michael Woodson

Michael Woodson
President

REPORTS

There are four common **report** formats:

- Memorandum report
- Letter report
- Short report
- Formal report

Memorandum Report

The **memorandum report** is a routine and informal report that might be prepared on a weekly basis to report the status of projects to upper management. This type of report:

- Is objective and impersonal in tone.
- May contain brief introductory comments.
- Contains headings and subheadings, used for quick reference and to highlight certain aspects of the report.
- Is usually single-spaced and printed on plain paper. (However, in some businesses this report may be sent as an email or email attachment.)

Letter Report

The **letter report** is normally a one-page letter that is printed on company letterhead. If the reports contain second sheets, the continuation pages are also printed on letterhead. The letter report:

- Is typically sent outside the company to consultants, clients, or the board of directors.
- Should have headings and subheadings to organize its content.

Short Report

The **short report** has a title page, a preliminary summary with conclusions and recommendations, authorization information, a statement of the problem, findings, conclusions, and recommendations. The short report:

■ May contain tables and graphs and can be either single- or double-spaced.

■ Contains headings and subheadings to organize the content and to emphasize certain aspects.

■ Has a title page with:

    ■ The report title (long titles are divided and centered)

    ■ The name, title, and address of the person or company to whom the report is being submitted

    ■ The preparer's name, title, and address

Formal Report

Included in the **formal report** are the:

■ Cover

■ Title page

■ Flyleaf

■ Title fly

■ Letter of authorization

■ Letter of transmittal

■ Foreword and/or prefaces

■ Acknowledgments

■ Table of contents

■ List of tables

■ List of figures

■ Synopsis

■ Body

■ Endnotes or footnotes

■ Appendix

■ Glossary

■ Bibliography

■ Index

When formatting your report, consider the following guidelines:

■ The margin settings for a formal report are:

    ■ First page's top margin—2 inches.

    ■ Subsequent pages' top margin—1 inch.

    ■ Bottom margins on all pages—1 inch.

    ■ The left and right margins on all pages—1 inch.

■ For bound reports, the left margin should be 1½ inches to allow extra room for the binding.

- The body of the report can be single- or double-spaced.

- Setoff quotations should be single-spaced, as are footnotes.

- Paragraph indentions should be five spaces.

- Long quotations should be indented five spaces from the left margin.

- Numbered and bullet lists should also be indented five spaces.

- Footnotes should match paragraph margins.

- Primary headings should be centered and bold, with additional space above and below.

- A 20- to 24-point sans serif font, such as Helvetica, should be used.

- Secondary headings should be aligned left justified, bold, with a 16- to 18-point sans serif font.

- Third-level headings should also be aligned left and bold, with 12- to 14-point sans serif font.

- There should be no page number on the title page, although a page number should be assigned for numbering purposes.

  - The front matter should use small Roman numerals (i, ii, iii, etc.) for numbering.

  - The body of the report should use Arabic numerals, starting with 1.

  - Page numbers should be either centered or in the right margin, either ½ to 1 inch from the top or ½ inch from the bottom.

Headings and subheadings should be parallel in structure.

Example of nonparallel structure:
1. Reading the Manual
2. The Instructions
3. How to Install the Software

Example of parallel structure:
1. Reading the Manual
2. Following the Instructions
3. Installing the Software

You should use a numbering system for headings. You can use numbers or a combination of numbers and letters.

Figure 63 shows two alternative heading numbering systems.

Figure 63 Heading Numbering Systems

System 1

1. Main Heading
   1.1 Subheading
   1.2 Subheading
       1.2.1 Third-level heading
       1.2.2 Third-level heading

System 2

I. Main Heading
   a. Subheading
   b. Subheading
       1. Third-level heading
       2. Third-level leading

The **cover** (Figure 64) should have the title and author's name, with the title printed in all capital letters.

The cover may be printed on card stock paper.

The **title page** should include:

■ The title of the report in all capitals and subtitle if there is one

■ The recipient's name, corporate title, department, company name, and address

■ The preparer's name, corporate title, department, company name, and address

■ The date the report is submitted

The **flyleaf** is a blank page that is inserted after the cover. It is also sometimes added to the end of the report just before the back cover.

The **title fly** is a single page with just the report title in all capitals, centered on the upper third of the page.

The **letter of authorization** should be printed on letterhead and explain who authorized the report and any specific details regarding the authorization.

The **letter of transmittal** (Figure 65) is a cover letter for the report. It explains the purpose of the report, the scope, limitations, reference materials, special comments, and acknowledgments.

The letter of transmittal may take the place of a **foreword** or **preface**.

The **acknowledgements** page should list individuals, companies, or institutions that assisted in creating the report.

The **table of contents** (Figure 66) should include headings, subheadings, and third-level headings with page numbers.

- You can use an outline style with a heading numbering system.

- If you are using a word processor, you can automatically generate a table of contents based on the heading styles.

If tables are used in the report, you should include a **list of tables** in the front matter. The list should include:

- Table numbers

- Page numbers

- The descriptions used as table titles in the body of the report

If illustrations are used in the report, you should include a **list of figures** (Figure 67) in the front matter. The list should include:

- Figure numbers

- Page numbers

- The captions used with the figures in the body of the report

The **body** of the report (Figure 68) should include:

- An introduction to the report.

- Introductions to the major sections—headings, subheadings, and third-level headings.

- A summary at the end of major sections.

■ Normal paragraph breaks, bullet lists, numbered lists, illustrations, and tables.

■ Footnotes or endnotes to present content that is not part of the main flow of the body.

■ Footnotes are short notes set at the bottom of the page.

■ Endnotes are placed at the end of the report.

Usually, footnotes or endnotes are numbered with a small, raised number ([1], [2], etc.) inserted at the end of the text, with the correspondingly numbered note at the bottom of the page or at the end of the report.

Footnotes and endnotes should include:

■ The author or author's names

■ The title of the source

■ The publisher

■ The date

■ A page reference

> **Example:** [1]Kevin Wilson and Jennifer Wauson, *The AMA Handbook of Business Documents* (New York, AMACOM Books, 2011), page 101.

Sometimes a footnote is used for just the first reference to a source. Then, in subsequent references, just the author names and the page number are listed.

> **Example:** Wilson and Wauson, 205.

Other parenthetical references are inserted in the text of the document inside parentheses.

If there are supplementary reference materials or sources of research—perhaps information that might be of interest to only some readers—you can include them at the end of the report in an **appendix**.

The **glossary** should include technical terms with definitions along with any abbreviations. In the body of the report, the abbreviations should be spelled out the first time they are used.

The **bibliography** lists:

■ All the sources of information used to compile the report

■ Research that was not cited as a footnote but used to create the report

The bibliography listings are ordered alphabetically by the authors' last names.

■ If there is no main author, then the book title is used.

■ The author's surname comes first.

■ Additional authors are listed first name, last name.

Example: Wilson, Kevin, and Jennifer Wauson. *The AMA Handbook of Business Documents* (New York, AMACOM Books, 2011).

An **index** is an option for many reports, and should be an alphabetical listing.

■ The first word of each entry has an initial capital letter, and the rest of the words are in lower case.

■ Subentries in the index are like subheadings and are indented one or two spaces.

■ Cross-references direct the reader to another location in the index.

(text continues on page 145)

Figure 64 Report Cover

ONLINE EMPLOYEE BENEFIT ELECTIONS

By:
Catherine Muncie
Muncie Consulting

Figure 65 Report Transmittal Letter

Muncie Consulting
1231 Peachtree Street
Atlanta, GA 30102

May 12, 2012

Mary Ann Cleveland
Vice President
Alstead Communications
3324 Interstate 75 Parkway
Atlanta, GA 30131

Dear Ms. Cleveland:

In accordance to our agreement for conducting research on alternatives to paper-based benefit elections, I am pleased to submit this report with my findings titled "Online Employee Benefit Elections."

The purpose of this report is provide information to the Alstead Communications Executive Board for the purpose of determining whether online employee self-service is a possibility for annual benefit elections. The report describes the online process and compares it to the current paper-based benefit election process. In addition, the report details various policies and controls that would need to be implemented in order to make online elections secure in order to protect sensitive personal information.

I hope you will find this report to be informative.
Respectfully yours,

Catherine Muncie

Catherine Muncie
Muncie Consulting

Encl: Report on Online Employee Benefit Elections

Figure 66 Report Table of Contents

TABLE OF CONTENTS

ii

Figure 67 Report List of figures

LIST OF FIGURES

Figure 68 Report Body

Report on
ONLINE EMPLOYEE BENEFIT ELECTIONS

I. Introduction

During the annual benefits enrollment period, benefits-eligible employees may make changes to their benefits or enroll in flexible spending accounts for the upcoming plan year.

New benefit elections are effective January 1–December 31 of the following year. Once Open Enrollment has concluded, employees may change their benefits during the plan year only if they experience a qualified status change (marriage, divorce, birth/adoption of a child, or death of a dependent).

The human resources department must complete a number of tasks during August and September in order to ensure the online forms are correct. These tasks include the following:

■ Determining wages for commissioned employees

■ Verifying employment status

■ Entering salary increases into the employee database

■ Updating employee addresses

1

REQUEST LETTERS

A **request letter** is written to seek information, permission, or an explanation. This type of letter should (Figure 69):

- Be courteous, tactful, brief, confident, and persuasive.

- Be straightforward and include as much detail as possible about the request.

- Not be overbearing or manipulative in trying to obtain the request.

    - Avoid apologizing for the request.

    - Make sure your request is reasonable.

- Make the reader feel complimented to be asked for a favor.

- Express your willingness to reciprocate.

- Invite the person to contact you with any questions or concerns.

Request letters are typically written to:

- Request a modification to an agreement.

- Request a document or publication.

- Seek a raise or promotion.

- Request a response to a survey.

- Ask for assistance.

- Request a discount.

- Ask for the correction of an error.

- Ask for a favor.

- Request a refund.

- Extend an invitation.

- Ask for more information.

- Request an estimate or bid.

Figure 69 Request Letter

May 8, 2012
Roswell News Weekly

3233 Alpharetta Highway
Roswell, GA 32311

Captain Larry Muncie
United States Air Force
Dobbins Air Force Base
Atlanta, GA 30223

Dear Captain Muncie:

This is a request under the Freedom of Information Act (5 U.S.C § 552).
I request that the following documents be provided to me:

1. Photographs of the B-29 airplane in the Dobbins Museum
2. Mission information for the B-29 airplane on display
3. Manufacturing information including when it was completed and
    what factory built the aircraft

To help you determine my status for the purpose of assessing fees,
you should know that I am a representative of the news media affiliated
with the *Roswell Weekly* newspaper, and this request is made as part
of news gathering, not for commercial use.

I am willing to pay the appropriate fees for this request up to a maximum
of $25. If you estimate that the fees will exceed this limit, please
contact me.

I have also included my telephone number and email address at which
I can be contacted if necessary to discuss any aspect of my request.

Sincerely,

Shelia Jefferson

Shelia Jefferson
Staff Reporter
(770) 555-1234
SJefferson@rosweekly.com

RESEARCH REPORT

Research reports summarize experimental findings and use additional reference sources to support the findings (Figure 70).

Research reports are commonly written in one of two ways:

- An argumentative research report makes a statement about a particular subject and then presents research to support the thesis.

- An analytical research report asks a question and then presents research describing various answers to the question.

A typical research report includes the following sections:

- Title page—a short 15-word-or-less description of the report

- Abstract—a short overview of the report that includes:
    - A statement of the problem
    - The study group
    - Dependent and independent variables
    - Research strategy
    - Major findings
    - Conclusions

- Introduction—a page that presents the investigated problem, explains the importance of the study, and supplies an overview of the research strategy

- Method—describing the sample, materials, and procedures used for the research (including all surveys, tests, questionnaires, interview forms, and laboratory equipment used in the research)

- Results—a summary of the findings from the research

- Discussion—an interpretation of the findings and the implications

- References—a list of sources used in the research

Figure 70 Analytical Research Report

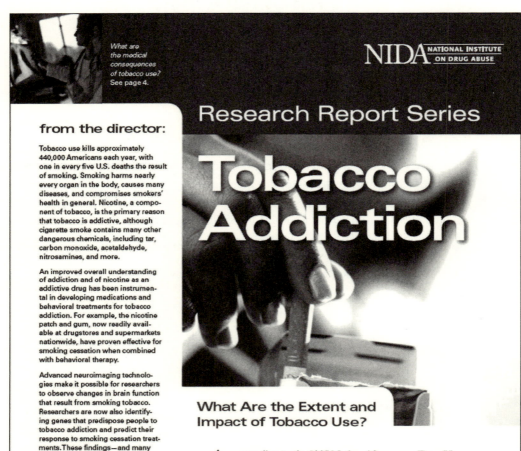

Research Report Series

Tobacco Addiction

to the Centers for Disease Control and Prevention there has been a decline of almost 50 percent since 1965.

NIDA's 2008 Monitoring the Future survey of 8th-, 10th-, and 12th-graders, which is used to track drug use patterns and attitudes, has also shown a striking decrease in smoking trends among the Nation's youth. The latest results indicate that about 7 percent of 8th-graders, 12 percent of 10th-graders, and 20 percent of 12th-graders had used cigarettes in the 30 days prior to the survey—the lowest levels in the history of the survey.

The declining prevalence of cigarette smoking among the general U.S. population, how-ever, is not reflected in patients with mental illnesses. The rate of smoking in patients suffering from post-traumatic stress disorder, bipolar disorder, major depression, and other mental illness is two- to fourfold higher than in the general population; and among people with schizophrenia, smoking rates as high as 90 percent have been reported.

Tobacco use is the leading preventable cause of death in the United States. The impact of tobacco use in terms of morbidity and mortality to society is staggering.

Economically, more than $96 billion of total U.S. health care costs each year are attributable directly to smoking.

However, this is well below the total cost to society because it does not include burn care from smoking-related fires, perinatal care for low-birthweight infants of mothers who smoke, and medical care costs associated with disease caused by secondhand smoke. In addition to health care costs, the costs of lost productivity due to smoking effects are estimated at $97 billion per year, bringing a conservative estimate of the economic burden of smoking to more than $193 billion per year.

How Does Tobacco Deliver Its Effects?

There are more than 4,000 chemicals found in the smoke of tobacco products. Of these, nicotine, first identified in the early 1800s, is the primary rein-forcing component of tobacco.

Cigarette smoking is the most popular method of using tobacco; however, there has also been a recent increase in the use of smokeless tobacco prod-ucts, such as snuff and chewing tobacco. These smokeless prod-ucts also contain nicotine, as well as many toxic chemicals.

The cigarette is a very efficient and highly engineered drug deliv-ery system. By inhaling tobacco smoke, the average smoker takes in 1–2 mg of nicotine per ciga-rette. When tobacco is smoked, nicotine rapidly reaches peak levels in the bloodstream and enters the brain. A typical smoker will take 10 puffs on a cigarette over a period of 5 minutes that

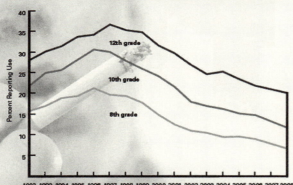

Trends in Prevalence of Cigarette Use for 8th-, 10th-, and 12th-Graders

Percentage of Students Using Cigarettes Over a 30-Day Period, 1992–2008

Source: University of Michigan, 2008 Monitoring the Future Survey.

RESIGNATION LETTER

A **resignation letter** becomes part of your personnel file and may be seen by future employers or if you reapply at the same organization. When writing a resignation letter, consider these tips (Figure 71):

- Highlight your accomplishments at the organization because your letter may be read by colleagues.

- Avoid emotion and maintain your dignity.

- Highlight your skills using action verbs.

- Emphasize the contributions you have made to the organization— be positive.

- Show enthusiasm and appreciation for what you have accomplished at the organization.

- The terms of your resignation should attempt to maintain a good relationship with your employer.

Resignation letters are typically written to:

- Resign from a job.

- Announce your retirement.

- Resign for health reasons.

- Resign to take another job.

- Resign for family reasons.

- Take early retirement.

Figure 71 Resignation Letter

Dorothy Speers
7877 Bells Ferry Road
Acworth, GA 30188
(770) 555-1212
DorothySpeers@abcd.com

September 1, 2012

Sally Duffey
Industrial Lighting Supply
4300 Westfield Highway
Cummings, GA 30134

Dear Ms. Duffey:

This letter is to announce my resignation from Industrial Lighting Supply, effective October 1, 2012.

I have enjoyed working for this company for the past five years, and it was a difficult decision to leave. I have enjoyed working with you and the rest of the sales department team. We accomplished a lot together. I am especially proud of the sales order system that I helped implement and for which I developed the training program.

I have accepted a position as general sales manager at Logan Manufacturing in Douglasville, Georgia. This is a great career opportunity for me, and it will reduce my morning commute substantially.

I wish you and everyone at Industrial Lighting Supply the very best.

Sincerely,

Dorothy Speers
Dorothy Speers

RÉSUMÉS

The purpose of a **résumé** to get the reader to give you an interview. A résumé should summarize and organize the information so that the reader understands that you are qualified for the job.

All résumés should include:

- Your name, address, and telephone number

- Educational background (schools attended, degrees, diplomas, special training)

- A listing of all previous employment:
  - The date, job title, and organization
  - A brief description of your job
  - *Not* salary

- Information about your current job:
  - Skills you have acquired
  - Your responsibilities

Optionally, a résumé can also contain:

- A job objective, which:
  - Should be tailored to each job for which you apply.
  - State the reason you are submitting your résumé for a particular job.

Example: To obtain a management position in human resources for a large communications firm that utilizes my leadership and organization skills

---

- Special skills, such as:
  - Software packages you've used
  - Languages you speak, read, and/or write

■ Professional association memberships

■ Honors and awards

Do not include references in your résumé. Instead, state that "References are available upon request." Have a list of references available with name, title, address, and phone number.

Use action verbs to describe your skills.

Example: Designed a new system to catch data entry errors.

Do not explain in your résumé why you are looking for a new job. Create several versions of your résumé, adapting the information to emphasize different skills required for different jobs. Emphasize your experience for various job possibilities.

There are two basic résumé formats:

■ The history (or chronological) format focuses on where you have worked (Figure 72).

■ The skills format lists skills you have acquired (Figure 73).

(text continues on page 156)

Figure 72 Chronological Format Résumé

Evelyn Flo Boyd
12345 Heartside Drive
Western Branch, GA 31234
404-555-1234

Experience

2009–Present   Lyon's Still Photography
                                                            Acworth, Georgia

Office manager and assistant to business owner
Maintained files and records, accounts receivable, and customer database.
Assisted photographer with photo subjects, as well as sales of proofs
and prints. Handled scheduling of business activities, all correspondence,
and travel arrangements.

1997–2009   Third Coast Video, Inc.
                                                               Austin, Texas

Office assistant
Scheduled clients and facilities for video production and postproduction
facility. Scheduled freelance crews and equipment rentals. Arranged
for shipping of equipment and travel for crews. Also handled invoicing
and correspondence.

Education
1993–1997: B.A. English
University of Texas
Austin, Texas

References furnished upon request.

Figure 73 Skills Format Résumé

Evelyn Flo Boyd
12345 Heartside Drive
Western Branch, GA 31234
404-555-1234

Experience

ADMINISTRATION—Maintained files and records, accounts receivable, and customer database. Handled scheduling of business activities, all correspondence, and travel arrangements.

SALES—Worked with customers to set appointments and to sell photography services.

VIDEO PRODUCTION—Coordinated scheduling of crews and facilities. Hired freelance crews and outline equipment rentals.

TECHNICAL SKILLS—Complete understanding of IBM-compatible software including Windows, Word for Windows, Excel, and WordPerfect. Also, some understanding of Apple Macintosh computers including Microsoft Word and Excel. Good typing skills, 50 wpm. Working knowledge of most office equipment, copiers, fax machines, and typewriters.

Work History
2009–Present
Office Manager and Assistant to Business Owner
Lyon's Still Photography
Acworth, Georgia

1997–2009
Office Assistant
Third Coast Video, Inc.
Austin, Texas

Education
1993-1997: B.A. English
University of Texas
Austin, Texas

References furnished upon request.

SALES LETTERS

Sales letters are written to catch the attention of readers in an attempt to sell them a product or service. When writing a sales letter, consider these tips (Figures 74 and 75):

A good sales letter focuses on what interests the readers:

- The benefits to the customer
- How the customer will use the product or service

If the letter is not personally addressed to the reader, start the letter with a headline that:

- Describes the key benefit to the reader.
- Uses power words such as *free, proven, imagine, how to, fast, cheap, save, enjoy,* and *introducing.*
- Gets the reader's attention, targets the audience, lists a benefit, and makes a promise.

  Example: How to save 50% or more on office furniture

If the letter is personally addressed, the opening sentence becomes the headline.

  Example: Dear Mr. Smith: How would you like to save 50% or more on office furniture for your business?

Keep the letter brief but interesting. Use short sentences, short paragraphs, bullet points, indented paragraphs, and subheadings to design the look of the letter and to make it visually attractive.

Start the letter by identifying the unique selling point of the product or service. Consider the following possibilities:

- Tell a story about the product or service and how it was used.
- Make an announcement of some important news about the product or service.
- Ask the reader a question that involves the unique selling point.
- Include a quotation from a testimonial.

- Include a celebrity endorsement.
- Provide surprising statistics to back up your claims.

Address the reader directly.

Incorrect: Many of you want . . .

Correct: You want . . .

Subheadings within the letter can be used to identify additional selling points.

Let the reader know how much the product or service costs.

The closing of the letter should include a call to action that asks for an order and explains how to order. The closing:

- May include a deadline.
- Always includes a thank-you.

Include a P.S. at the end of the letter to offer an incentive, sale, free trial, or gift. People often read a P.S.

Sales letters are typically written to:

- Announce a sale or a sales-related contest.
- Contact customers who have been inactive for a while.
- Send a thank-you note to an existing customer.
- Introduce a new catalog or product.
- Offer gifts and incentives to customers.
- Invite a customer to request a sample.
- Make an appointment for a sales presentation.
- Respond to customer inquiries.
- Solicit mail order purchases.
- Welcome a new customer.
- Strengthen a relationship with an existing customer.

(text continues on page 160)

Figure 74 Sales Letter

Business Furniture Liquidators
1245 North Main Street
Atlanta, Georgia 30322
December 1, 2012

Martha Sanchez
First Insurance
3211 Lake Tarn Terrace
Acworth, GA 30188

Dear Ms. Sanchez:

How would you like to save up to 75% on name-brand office furniture? Business Furniture Liquidators specializes in preowned Herman Miller and Steelcase desks and chairs. Why pay full price for new office furniture when you can get quality refurbished furniture at up to 75% off?

Are you planning to expand your business or upgrade your existing offices? Business Furniture Liquidators can help you design and furnish offices, reception areas, and conference rooms. We have a network of distributors throughout the southeast that allow us to offer you a wide range of choices at a price you can afford. We'll personally deliver and install your furniture to ensure your satisfaction.

Visit our Web site at www.bfl.com or call us at 1-800-555-1212 to request a free quote. You'll find daily specials on our Web site and pictures of our latest offerings.

Sincerely,

Warren Gladson

Warren Gladson
1-800-555-1212
Wgladson@blf.com
www.blf.com

P.S. For the month of December we are having a liquidation sale on all Herman Miller office chairs. This is a great opportunity for you to upgrade your office chairs to ergonomically friendly Herman Miller chairs at 80% off the retail price. Call or email me today for an inventory list and a price quote.

Figure 75 Sales Letter

Realty Investors
7788 Princeton Avenue
St. Louis, MO 63107

Do you have a house you would like to sell?

Dear Homeowner,

Do you own a home in St. Louis that you would like to sell? If so,
we would like to meet with you to discuss some great opportunities.

Realty Investors specializes in helping investors find great opportunities
in rental properties. We work with a large network of investors who are
interested in purchasing rental properties. If you are interested in selling
your property, now is a great time to talk to us and let us help you get
the best price possible.

Last year, we helped our investors purchase over $20 million in properties
in the St. Louis metro area and this year we will easily exceed that
amount.

Here is a list of properties our investors are looking for:

- Single-family, 2- or 3-bedroom homes priced under $150,000

- Duplexes with 2 bedrooms and 1 bath on each side

- Mobile homes

- Two-story homes of any size

If you own a property like one of these, please give me a call and let me
conduct a property evaluation. There's no obligation to sell, and the evaluation is completely free.

Selling your property with Realty Investors is an outstanding opportunity.

I look forward to hearing from you.

Sincerely,

Bill Stovall

Bill Stovall
(314) 555-1212

SEASONAL CORRESPONDENCE

Seasonal correspondence is a way of greeting customers and employees by writing holiday letters (Figure 76). Holiday letters to customers can include special offers and incentives with deadlines related to the holiday.

These letters to customers may also express appreciation for past business. When writing a holiday letter to customers, consider these tips:

- Greet the customer.
- Acknowledge the upcoming holiday.
- Describe the offer.
- Express appreciation for the customer's business.
- Close by offering warm wishes.

Holiday letters to employees can be used to express thanks for their hard work. When writing holiday letters to employees, consider these tips:

- Begin with a personal greeting.
- Acknowledge the upcoming holiday.
- Mention it in the letter if it includes a bonus or gift check.
- Announce any holiday parties, and include information about the date, time, location, and whether there is a need to RSVP.
- Include any messages about company accomplishments for the latest period and any goals for the future.
- Close by wishing the employee a happy holiday.

Holiday letters are most effective when they are personally addressed to the reader. Be sensitive to the fact that the individual may not celebrate the holiday.

Holiday letters are typically written to:

- Announce a holiday-related sale.
- Thank customers for their previous business.
- Announce a holiday-related open house.
- Announce a party.
- Offer season's greetings.
- Announce a holiday schedule.

Figure 76 Seasonal Correspondence

Acme Auto Supply
5353 Buffalo Speedway
Houston, TX 77097

December 7, 2012

Jeff Richardson
Jeff's Auto Repair
3221 Stella Link
Houston, TX 77098

Dear Mr. Richardson,

With the holiday season approaching, there is so much personal and business activity to take care of that it is sometimes easy to forget to thank our great customers who have helped make it a great year for us.

I want to personally thank you for your business and for being a loyal customer of Acme Auto Supply.

May this holiday season bring happiness to you and your family.

Very truly yours,

Sam Henderson

Sam Henderson
(713) 555-1212

SPECIFICATIONS

Specifications appear in various forms—the design of high-tech products, software development, engineering, and architecture (Figure 77). Specifications dictate the design of the project. They describe how the product should appear when completed. They can be included as part of a contract.

There are four major types of specifications:

- Requirement specifications (architecture and engineering) describe:
    - A product during the design phase
    - The functions the product will be capable of performing
    - The costs involved in making the product
- Functional specifications (manufacturing) describe:
    - The purpose, use, and operation of the product
    - How the components work together
    - The electronics that will be used
    - The power requirements
    - The production and maintenance costs
- Design specifications (software) describe:
    - The documents that contain information about the product
    - The product's functions, what it does, and how it does it
    - Any external components that interface with the product
    - The details of all the products' functions
    - The power requirements
- Test specifications (manufacturing and software) describe:
    - All the tests that will be run on the product during the development phase
    - All the tests that will be run on the production version of the product.

When writing specifications, keep the following language usage guidelines in mind:

- Keep sentences short and simple.

- Edit carefully to avoid mistakes that cause errors in the interpretation of the specifications and that result in manufacturing or development mistakes.

- Reference other documents and paragraphs rather than repeat content.

- Don't worry about repeating the same words and phrases.

- Use caution with ambiguous words like *any, include,* and *run.*

- Define acronyms the first time they are used.

- Avoid the use of words that may create logic errors in the specifications.

   Example: all, always, never, every, none

- Do not use slash marks in specifications.

   Incorrect: A/B

   Correct: either A or B

- Use verbs in the future tense, using the emphatic form such as *shall.*

   - *Shall* expresses a requirement.

   - *Will, should,* and *may* do not express a requirement.

- Describe the person who will be using the product in the specifications.

   Example: The operator will be a licensed engineer.

- Be specific when using noun modifiers that could be interpreted to apply to two or more nouns.

   Incorrect: The cabin door will be connected to the doorway using metal pins and lock pins made of titanium.

   Correct: The cabin door will be connected to the doorway using titanium pins and titanium lock pins.

- Use caution when writing essential and nonessential dependent clauses with words like *that* and *which*.

  - Essential clauses are required to specify a particular item and are often introduced by *that*.

  - Nonessential clauses are not required to specify anything and are often introduced using *which*.

  - Other introductory words that introduce essential and nonessential clauses are *after, as, as if, as though, as soon as, at which, because, before, by which, for which, if, in order that, since, so that, to which, unless, when, where, which, while, who, whom,* and *whose*.

- Avoid using multiple conjunctions in the same sentence.

  Incorrect: The cabin door will be sealed by gluing and clamping or riveting.

  Correct: The cabin door will be sealed either by gluing and clamping or by riveting.

- Use the third person.

  Incorrect: You will push the green on-screen **Start** button to begin the test.

  Correct: The operator will push the green on-screen **Start** button to begin the test.

- When including lists in specifications, make sure they are complete and parallel in structure.

  - The elements of the list should be the same part of speech.

Figure 77 Specifications

STUDENT COMPUTER SPECIFICATIONS

All students are required to have a desktop or laptop computer as well as a printer for use throughout the school year. Computers must also include a three-year on-site warranty for parts and labor, as well as telephone or Internet support.

Operating System

- Windows 7

Software Suite

- Microsoft Office Professional with Word, Excel, PowerPoint, and Outlook
- Internet Explorer browser
- Norton Antivirus

Computer Hardware

- Processor speed of at least 2 GHz
- Memory (RAM) of 2 GB or more
- Hard disk drive of at least 100 GB
- DVD burner CD-RW combo disc drive
- 19-inch flat panel display
- Inkjet printer and printer cable plus three additional sets of replacement ink cartridges
- 10/100Base-T Ethernet card or wireless Ethernet card
- USB Flash memory stick with at least 1 GB of capacity
- Multimedia sound capability
- Headphones

SPEECHES AND ORAL PRESENTATIONS

Writing a **speech** involves writing a script that can be memorized or read from a teleprompter, as well as speaker notes that the speaker can refer to during the presentation. (Figure 78.)

In *planning* a speech, keep the following in mind:

- Is the purpose of the speech to inform, instruct, or persuade?
  - An informational speech focuses on facts.
  - An instructional speech explains how to do something.
  - A persuasive speech attempts to convince the audience to think and act a certain way.
- Consider the audience for the speech and the location.
  - The audience and location will affect the tone of the speech.
  - Consider what the members of the audience have in common, such as age, interests, gender, and ethnicity.
  - Consider how much the audience already knows about the topic.
    - Will they already be familiar with the content, or will you be introducing new ideas?
    - What level of detail is appropriate for the audience?
    - What might offend the audience?
- Plan the presentation to avoid standing behind a podium.
  - Walk around but don't pace.
  - Plan on addressing different parts of the audience rather than one or two people in the front row.
- Determine whether accompanying visuals are appropriate. They may be appropriate depending on the audience and location.

In *writing* a speech, consider the following:

- Write a good introduction that gives a short overview and creates interest.
    - Create a hook that captures the audience's attention.
        - Offer shocking statistics.
        - Ask a thought-provoking question.
- Establish the reason you are speaking and why your topic is important.
    - Describe the topic from the audience's point of view.
- Divide your speech into sections, and give each section a verbal title.
- Use summaries and logical transitions to move from one section to the next.
    - Repeat crucial points to remind the audience.
    - Repeat crucial buzzwords to reinforce their meaning.
    - Use powerful transitions to reinforce or contrast ideas.
- Write the speech with short uncomplicated sentences.
    - Avoid using too many subordinate clauses.
    - Avoid the use of too many pronouns; it is hard for an audience to remember who and what *it, they,* and *this* mean.
- Use the strategies of ethos, pathos, and logos.
    - Ethos builds trust between the speaker and the audience.
    - Pathos appeals to the audience's emotions.
    - Logos provides facts, statistics, and logic.
- Conclude the speech by summarizing, stating your own conclusion, and then adding last thoughts as commentary.
    - Restate the main points of the speech, but don't repeat them the same way they were originally delivered.
    - End with a call to action that creates a connection with the audience.

(text continues on page 172)

Figure 78 Speech by John F. Kennedy

ASK NOT WHAT YOUR COUNTRY CAN DO FOR YOU
By John F. Kennedy

Vice President Johnson, Mr. Speaker, Mr. Chief Justice, President Eisenhower, Vice President Nixon, President Truman, reverend clergy, fellow citizens, we observe today not a victory of party, but a celebration of freedom—symbolizing an end, as well as a beginning—signifying renewal, as well as change. For I have sworn before you and Almighty God the same solemn oath our forebears prescribed nearly a century and three quarters ago.

The world is very different now. For man holds in his mortal hands the power to abolish all forms of human poverty and all forms of human life. And yet the same revolutionary beliefs for which our forebears fought are still at issue around the globe—the belief that the rights of man come not from the generosity of the state, but from the hand of God.

We dare not forget today that we are the heirs of that first revolution. Let the word go forth from this time and place, to friend and foe alike, that the torch has been passed to a new generation of Americans—born in this century, tempered by war, disciplined by a hard and bitter peace, proud of our ancient heritage—and unwilling to witness or permit the slow undoing of those human rights to which this Nation has always been committed, and to which we are committed today at home and around the world.

Let every nation know, whether it wishes us well or ill, that we shall pay any price, bear any burden, meet any hardship, support any friend, oppose any foe, in order to assure the survival and the success of liberty.

This much we pledge—and more.

To those old allies whose cultural and spiritual origins we share, we pledge the loyalty of faithful friends. United, there is little we cannot do in a host of cooperative ventures. Divided, there is little we can do—for we dare not meet a powerful challenge at odds and split asunder.

To those new States whom we welcome to the ranks of the free, we pledge our word that one form of colonial control shall not have passed away merely to be replaced by a far more iron tyranny. We shall not always expect to find them supporting our view. But we shall always hope to find them strongly supporting their own freedom—and to remember that, in the past, those who foolishly sought power by riding the back of the tiger ended up inside.

To those peoples in the huts and villages across the globe struggling to break the bonds of mass misery, we pledge our best efforts to help them help themselves, for whatever period is required—not because the Communists may be doing it, not because we seek their votes, but because it is right. If a free society cannot help the many who are poor, it cannot save the few who are rich.

To our sister republics south of our border, we offer a special pledge—to convert our good words into good deeds—in a new alliance for progress—to assist free men and free governments in casting off the chains of poverty. But this peaceful revolution of hope cannot become the prey of hostile powers. Let all our neighbors know that we shall join with them to oppose aggression or subversion anywhere in the Americas. And let every other power know that this Hemisphere intends to remain the master of its own house.

To that world assembly of sovereign states, the United Nations, our last best hope in an age where the instruments of war have far outpaced the instruments of peace, we renew our pledge of support—to prevent it from becoming merely a forum for invective—to strengthen its shield of the new and the weak—and to enlarge the area in which its writ may run.

Finally, to those nations who would make themselves our adversary, we offer not a pledge but a request: that both sides begin anew the quest for peace, before the dark powers of destruction unleashed by science engulf all humanity in planned or accidental self-destruction.

We dare not tempt them with weakness. For only when our arms are sufficient beyond doubt can we be certain beyond doubt that they will never be employed.

(continues)

Figure 78 *(continued)*

But neither can two great and powerful groups of nations take comfort from our present course—both sides overburdened by the cost of modern weapons, both rightly alarmed by the steady spread of the deadly atom, yet both racing to alter that uncertain balance of terror that stays the hand of mankind's final war.

So let us begin anew—remembering on both sides that civility is not a sign of weakness, and sincerity is always subject to proof. Let us never negotiate out of fear. But let us never fear to negotiate.

Let both sides explore what problems unite us instead of belaboring those problems which divide us.

Let both sides, for the first time, formulate serious and precise proposals for the inspection and control of arms—and bring the absolute power to destroy other nations under the absolute control of all nations.

Let both sides seek to invoke the wonders of science instead of its terrors. Together let us explore the stars, conquer the deserts, eradicate disease, tap the ocean depths, and encourage the arts and commerce.

Let both sides unite to heed in all corners of the earth the command of Isaiah—to "undo the heavy burdens—and to let the oppressed go free."

And if a beachhead of cooperation may push back the jungle of suspicion, let both sides join in creating a new endeavor, not a new balance of power, but a new world of law, where the strong are just and the weak secure and the peace preserved.

All this will not be finished in the first 100 days. Nor will it be finished in the first 1,000 days, nor in the life of this Administration, nor even perhaps in our lifetime on this planet. But let us begin.

In your hands, my fellow citizens, more than in mine, will rest the final success or failure of our course. Since this country was founded, each generation of Americans has been summoned to give testimony to its national loyalty. The graves of young Americans who answered the call to service surround the globe.

Now the trumpet summons us again—not as a call to bear arms, though arms we need; not as a call to battle, though embattled we are—but a call to bear the burden of a long twilight struggle, year in and year out, "rejoicing in hope, patient in tribulation"—a struggle against the common enemies of man: tyranny, poverty, disease, and war itself.

Can we forge against these enemies a grand and global alliance, North and South, East and West, that can assure a more fruitful life for all mankind? Will you join in that historic effort?

In the long history of the world, only a few generations have been granted the role of defending freedom in its hour of maximum danger. I do not shrink from this responsibility—I welcome it. I do not believe that any of us would exchange places with any other people or any other generation. The energy, the faith, the devotion which we bring to this endeavor will light our country and all who serve it—and the glow from that fire can truly light the world.

And so, my fellow Americans: ask not what your country can do for you—ask what you can do for your country.

My fellow citizens of the world: ask not what America will do for you, but what together we can do for the freedom of man.

Finally, whether you are citizens of America or citizens of the world, ask of us the same high standards of strength and sacrifice which we ask of you. With a good conscience our only sure reward, with history the final judge of our deeds, let us go forth to lead the land we love, asking His blessing and His help, but knowing that here on earth God's work must truly be our own.

SUMMARIES

Summary writing is a way of organizing and summarizing information that condenses large quantities of information into a shorter version that can be used for easy reference.

In technical writing, summary writing is employed to create abstracts, which provide a brief overview of a document.

To write summaries or abstracts, do the following (Figure 79):

- Read the longer document thoroughly, and make sure you completely understand the content.

- Review the longer document a second time, and strike out material that you feel isn't necessary and underline the most important points.

- Write a summary in your own words, following the organization of the original material.

- Mention the author, title, and publication date.

- Avoid unnecessary details and quotes.

- Don't give your own opinion.

- Any material used verbatim from the original should be properly documented.

- Compare your draft summary with the original for accuracy.

- The finished summary should be no longer than 20% of the original's length.

(text continues on page 176)

Figure 79 Summary

ENERGY AND ECONOMIC IMPACTS OF IMPLEMENTING BOTH
A 25-PERCENT RPS AND A 25-PERCENT RFS BY 2025

1. Background and Scope of the Analysis

Background

This Service Report was prepared by the Energy Information Administration (EIA) in response to a request from Senator James Inhofe.[5] Senator Inhofe requested an analysis of a proposal (referred to as the 25 × 25 Policy Scenario in his letter request) to achieve a 25-percent renewable portfolio standard (RPS) and a 25-percent renewable fuel standard (RFS) by 2025. The combined RPS and RFS policy proposal is referred to as "the Policy" hereafter in the report. Copies of the request letter and a follow-up letter of clarification are provided in Appendix A.

Proposal Summary

The proposal analyzed in this study has two components: (1) an RPS, which requires that the percentage of electricity sales produced from renewable sources, excluding existing hydroelectric generation, must reach 25 percent by 2025; and (2) an RFS, which requires that the volumetric percentage of the transportation gasoline and diesel fuel market supplied from renewable resources, in the form of ethanol and biodiesel, must reach 25 percent by 2025 and then grow proportionately with growth in demand for transportation gasoline and diesel fuel. Each sector (electricity sales and gasoline plus diesel transport fuels) is required to meet its own target by 2025. Twenty-five percent of electricity sales would be from renewable generators and 25 percent of gasoline plus diesel fuel sales would be from either ethanol or biodiesel on a volumetric basis.

A key assumption in both the electricity and transportation sectors is that all tax or other policy incentives for domestic renewable fuels and ethanol import tariffs in current laws and regulations are allowed to sunset without extension.

The RPS target in the electricity sector is implemented using a credit trading system, where the qualifying renewables include:

(Courtesy of the U.S. Department of Energy)

(continues)

Figure 79 *(continued)*

- Biomass used in dedicated plants or co-fired with other fuels

- Geothermal

- Municipal solid waste (including landfill gas)

- Solar thermal

- Photovoltaic (PV)

- Wind (both onshore and offshore)

- Incremental new hydroelectricity above that existing in 2006

Further, existing qualifying generators, except existing hydroelectricity, receive credits under the proposed Policy. The renewable share is expressed as a share of electricity sales in kilowatt hours. The required share is set equal to the share of qualifying renewable generation sales in 2006 and increases to 25 percent in 2025. Thereafter, it is held at 25 percent. All retail electricity sellers are included. RPS credit trading is allowed only within the electricity sector, and there is no cap on the credit price.

The RFS target for the motor transportation sector is also implemented using tradable credits, where the qualifying renewable fuels include:

- Corn-based ethanol

- Cellulose-based ethanol

- Biodiesel production from all sources, including animal fats and oil-based beans/seeds

As with the RPS, existing qualifying sources receive credits. The renewable share is expressed as a share of all liquids sold in the motor transportation sector that displace either gasoline or diesel. The required share is set equal to the share of qualifying renewables sold in 2006 and increases to 25 percent in 2025. Thereafter, it is held at 25 percent. RFS credit trading is allowed only within the transportation sector, and there is no cap on the credit price. The existing import tariff on Brazilian ethanol imports (51 cents per gallon) is allowed to sunset in 2010. Finally, measures that facilitate compliance with the RFS, such as mandates to produce Flex Fuel Vehicles (FFVs) and the availability of E85 pumps at gasoline dispensing stations, are assumed as stipulated in Senate Bill 23 (S.23).

General Methodology

In this study, analyses of the energy sector impacts and energy-related economic impacts of the Policy proposal are based on the Annual Energy Outlook 2007 (AEO2007)[6] reference and high price cases, as amended to allow for the additional assumptions and modeling enhancements necessary to evaluate the proposal. As in the preparation of the Annual Energy Outlook and most EIA service reports, the National Energy Modeling System (NEMS) was used to evaluate the impacts of the Policy Case and alternative assumptions.

A number of changes were made in NEMS to address the Policy and to include enhancements relevant to the analysis. They included changes to the macroeconomic module to improve the representation of the impact on the entire economy of price increases for agricultural products, motor fuel, and electricity; changes in the Petroleum Market Module to ensure convergence of NEMS; and changes to the Renewable Fuels and Transportation Modules to incorporate the proposal's mandates. The changes made to the AEO2007 NEMS are summarized in Appendix B.

Sensitivity Cases

In addition to the four cases requested by Senator Inhofe (Reference, High Price, Policy, and High Price Policy), four additional cases are provided to illustrate the impacts of higher availability of ethanol imports and more optimistic assumptions for the cellulosic ethanol technology: Low-Cost Ethanol Imports, Low-Cost Ethanol Imports Policy, High Renewable Technology, and High Renewable Technology Policy. The cases analyzed for this request are shown in Table 1. High Renewable Technology and High Technology are used interchangeably throughout this text.

TERMINATION OF EMPLOYMENT LETTER

A **termination of employment letter** is an official announcement regarding a layoff or firing. A termination letter should come at the end of a termination process that involves personnel meetings.

Termination letters are usually written because of redundancy in positions, misconduct by an employee, or poor performance.

A termination of employment letter should (Figure 80):

- Be courteous and professional.

- Start by announcing the termination and the effective date.

- State the reasons for the termination.

- Clearly state any individual requirements, such as the return of a company car, credit card, computer, or cell phone.

- Clearly state any details regarding pay, holiday pay, benefits, pension, and other financial settlement.

- Describe the appeals process and schedule if an appeals process is required due to state law or union contract.

- Include a place for the employee to sign to confirm receipt of the letter.

Figure 80 Termination Letter

Credit Corp America
4300 Interstate Parkway
Dallas, TX 75301
September 6, 2012

Mary Sullivan
6426 Lakewood Blvd
Dallas, TX 75214

Dear Mrs. Sullivan:

As we discussed in our meeting on September 5, 2012, I regretfully must inform you that your employment with Credit Corp America will be terminated today, September 6, 2012.

As described in our meeting, the reason for termination of your employment is your failure to meet your sales quotas. You failed to meet your monthly quota three months ago and were given a warning at that time. You have continued to miss your quota for each of the past three months.

As part of the termination process, you must return your sales literature, customer lists, and company laptop.

You will receive two weeks' pay, which will be sent to your home within the next five days. You will also retain your 401(k) account. Your health insurance benefits will continue through the end of September. At that time, you have the option of continuing your coverage by purchasing it through the COBRA program.

To acknowledge your receipt of this letter, please sign and date below and return it to me.

We are sorry to see you leave and wish you the best for the future.

Yours,

Mary Ann Lemer

Mary Ann Lemer
Vice President of Sales

I acknowledge receipt of this letter.

_____   _____

Mary Sullivan   Date

TRAINING MANUAL

Training manuals are designed to instruct the reader on how to do something. There are two main types of training manuals:

- **Instructor-led manuals** may rely on lectures and demonstrations by the instructor (Figure 81).

- **Self-paced training manuals** must provide more instructions than an instructor-led manual (Figure 82).

A typical training manual includes:

- Cover (Figure 83)

- Table of contents (Figure 84)

- How-to-get-started information (Figure 85)

- Lesson modules

- Appendix items

- Glossary

- End-of-course quiz (Figure 86)

- Course evaluation form (Figure 87)

Training manuals are normally divided into lessons or topics. A typical lesson includes:

- Lesson overview and objectives (Figure 88–89)

- Explanation in the form of headings, subheadings, paragraphs of text, and lists

- Illustrations, diagrams, charts, screen captures, or photographs.

- Tables (Figure 90)

■ Step-by-step instructions (Figure 91)

■ Use of bold, italics, and all caps to highlight actions to be taken by the participant

■ Exercises (Figure 92)

■ Quizzes

■ Summaries

Instructor-led manuals may include:

■ Copies of PowerPoint slides used by the instructor as visual aids

■ Speaker notes that summarize the instructor's lecture

■ Speaker notes in the participant's version of the manual

Notes and warning messages may be formatted with icons and graphic boxes to focus the student's attention.

Training manuals may be integrated with other forms of instruction, such as:

■ Hands-on exercises

■ Team exercises

■ Exercises involving online simulations

■ Videos and audio recordings

■ Computer-based training

■ Webinars

■ Job aids

(text continues on page 192)

Figure 81 Instructor-Led Training Manual

Module 3: Reviewing Financial Statements

Topic 1:
Traditional Financial Statements

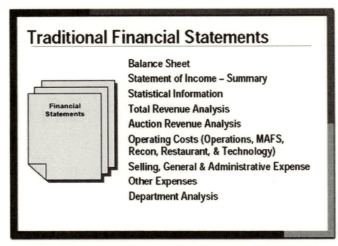

Traditional financial statements include information such as the current month, prior year, budget, year-to-date, and variance percentages. The traditional financial statements include:

- Balance Sheet
- Statement of Income – Summary
- Statistical Information
- Total Revenue Analysis
- Auction Revenue Analysis
- Operating Costs (Operations, MAFS, Recon, Restaurant, & Technology)
- Selling, General & Administrative Expense
- Other Expenses
- Department Analysis (One Statement of Income for each Department)

The Department Analysis provides the detail of revenues and expenses, gross profit, gross profit margin, IBD, and IBD Margin for each department and/or profit center, thus providing a basis to analyze operational performance by type of service.

Figure 82 Self-Study Training Manual

Managing Performance Everyday

PERFORMANCE EVALUATION FORMS

For recording your written performance evaluation, Manheim has three Performance Expectations and Review forms:

- Employee form

- Managers, Supervisors, and Professional form

- Basic form

Goals

Page one of the form includes space for writing the goals for the year along with the tracking method. The first page should have been completed at the beginning of the review period. During the evaluation, you will determine if the goals were achieved. There are four possible ratings for each goal on the form: exceeded, met, did not meet, and not applicable.

Goals for the Review Period

Identify three goals to be accomplished during the review period by thinking of the key responsibilities for this job. At the end of the performance period, rate how well these goals were achieved.

Goals for the Review Period Make goals SMART: Specific, Measurable, Attainable, Realistic, and Timely	Tracking Method How we know it was achieved	Were the goals achieved?			
		Exceeded	Met	Did Not	N/A
1 Maintain current Cust Sat Rating of 98%	Customer Survey	○	●	○	○
2 Increase dealer use of Recon Services over current level	Recon Sales Report	●	○	○	○
3 Increase dealer sales percentage by 5%	Dealer Sales Report	○	○	●	○

Page 10

Part 3
Participant Guide

Figure 83 Training Manual Cover

PART 3:
Evaluate for Performance

Training Guide

Figure 84 Training Manual Table of Contents

Table of Contents

Figure 85 Training Manual Getting-Started Page

How to Take a Self Study Course

Welcome to Finance Training Self Study

This self study course allows you to learn independently and at your own pace. It contains many learning elements including a written presentation, associated activities, and online simulations and practices.

How to Take This Course

Study the written documentation and complete the associated activities, online simulations and online practice exercises.

Once you complete the course, you must register for the associated quiz on LMS and pass with an 80% or greater to receive credit for the self study.

Online Simulations:

Throughout the self study course, you will be able to watch demonstrations and then practice the same concepts in a simulated environment.

Self study online simulations allow you to view content in either See It! or Try It! mode.

Mode	Name	Description
	See It!	See It mode enables you to learn about the selected topic by displaying an animated demonstration of a task being completed.
	Try It!	Try It mode allows you to perform the selected task in a simulated environment

Steps to run simulations and practice exercises:

1. Access online simulations through the website and select the **Online Simulations** link.

2. Next, select the module you're studying.

3. This will launch the simulation player in a new window.

4. From this window, choose the topic you'd like to view in either See it! or Try it! mode.

Figure 86 Training Manual Quiz

Managing Performance Everyday

Quiz
Which Rating Error Are They Making?

1. Bob's latest project was great. He did miss on projects in the first half of the year, but he turned around nicely. I'm going to rate him exceeded expectations.

    a. Rating effort rather than performance

    b. Recent work focus (Recency Effect)

    c. Halo or horns effect

2. Stan made some people upset in the process, but he did get the job done. I'm going to rate him exceeded expectations.

    a. No news is good news

    b. Halo or horns effect

    c. Central tendency

3. Sara is one of my best friends, even though her performance is falling. I'm going to rate her meets expectations.

    a. Interpersonal relations bias

    b. Just like me or not like me

    c. Judging by association

4. There are no superstars in by book.

    a. Central tendency

    b. Judging by association

    c. Strictness

5. Janice and I used to work together at another company. We both understand what it takes to get ahead in this world.

    a. Leniency

    b. Just like me or not like me

    c. Central tendency

Figure 87 Training Manual Course Evaluation

Module 6: Activities

Participant Feedback Survey

Please take a moment to complete the following survey. We are interested in learning about your experience with this course.

Instructor's Name

_____

Instructions

Please answer the questions below by circling the appropriate number on the right.

Scale

Strongly Disagree 1..2..3..4..5 Strongly Agree

1) I feel comfortable working with financial statements,	1..2..3..4..5
2) I feel comfortable finding information within the balance sheet.	1..2..3..4..5
3) I feel comfortable finding information within the statement of income.	1..2..3..4..5
4) I feel comfortable finding trends and other relationships within the financial statement data.	1..2..3..4..5
5) This course has taught me skills I need in my job,	1..2..3..4..5
6) The instructor effectively presented the course,	1..2..3..4..5
7) The instructor provided answers to my questions,	1..2..3..4..5

Figure 88   Training Manual Course Objectives

INTRODUCTION AND COURSE AGENDA

Welcome to the third module of Managing Performance Everyday. In this course, Evaluate for Performance, you will learn how to effectively evaluate performance and get prepared to confidently and respectfully discuss with your employees their performance and upcoming goals.

Performance Management Cycle

- **Set Goals** or expectations with your employees.

- **Feedback** is ongoing and lets employees know how they are doing and reinforces what the manager expects from the employee every day.

- **Track** how employees are doing against their goals.

- **Coach** the employee to make improvements.

- **Evaluate** the employee's performance on how they did against their goals and set new goals for next year.

Figure 89 Training Manual Lesson Contents and Objectives

Module 4
Accounting for Holds Roll-Forward Transactions

This module focuses on the accounting procedures for Holds Roll-Forward transactions.

Module Objectives

This module explains:

- How to perform the accounting entries necessary to perform Holds Roll-Forward

Module Contents

This module contains the following topics:

Figure 90 Training Manual Table Reference

Oracle Forms Icons

	Icons	
Icon	**Name**	**Description**
	New	Creates a new record in the active form.
	Find	Displays the Find window to retrieve records.
	Show Navigator	Displays the Navigator window.
	Save	Saves any pending changes in the active form.
	Switch Responsibility	Allows you to select another Responsibility if you have more than one Responsibility.
	Print	Prints the current screen that the cursor is in. In some cases it may print a report associated with the current data.
	Close Form	Closes all windows of the current form.
	Cut	Cuts the current selection to the clipboard.
	Copy	Copies the current selection to the clipboard.
	Paste	Pastes from the clipboard into the current field.
	Clear Record	Erases the current record from the window.
	Delete	Deletes the current record from the database.
	Edit Field	Displays the Editor window for the current field.
	Zoom	Displays custom-defined Zoom (drilldown behavior).
	Attachments	Displays the Attachment window.
?	Window Help	Displays help for the current window.

Figure 91 Training Manual Instructions

Changing Preference Settings

1. Log in to the application.

2. In the Applications Home Page, click **Preferences**.

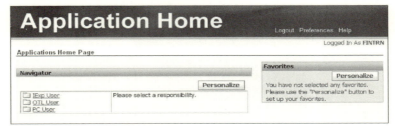

3. The **General Preferences** page is displayed.

4. *Date Format:* Change it to the desired format.

5. *Timezone:* Change it your time zone.

6. Click **Apply**.

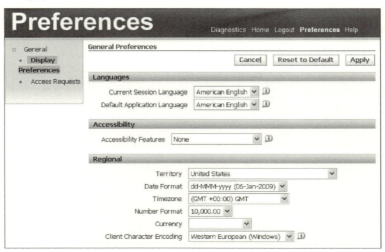

7. Verify that the message **Confirmation. Updated successfully.** appears at the top of the screen.

Figure 92 Training Manual Group Activity

Financial Statement Review	Higher Up Increased	Lower Down Decreased
1 Are the YTD revenues for the location up or down when compared to prior year?	☐	☐
2 What revenue category has increased the most on a YTD basis when compared to prior year?	_____	
3 What revenue category has decreased the most on a YTD basis when compared to prior year?	_____	
4 Are the YTD Operating expenses up or down over last year?	☐	☐
5 Are the YTD SG&A expenses up or down over last year?	☐	☐
6 What category of Reconditioning revenue has had the greatest % change over prior year to date?	_____	
7 How many sale days did the location have in the most recent month?	_____	
8 What expense category (Operating or SG&A) has had the greatest percent change when compared to the prior year?	_____	
9 How many cars did the location register in most current month?	_____	
10 What was the average registration per sale in most current month?	_____	
11 How many cars did the location sell in most current month?	_____	
12 What was the location's sales ratio for most current month?	_____	
13 Was the location's sales ratio for current month higher or lower than the prior year?	☐	☐
14 Was the location's sales ratio for current month higher or lower than YTD for the prior year?	☐	☐

TRIP REPORT

A **trip report** is usually a simple memo that is sent to a supervisor after an employee returns from a business trip.

A trip report should include (Figure 93):

- The purpose of the trip
- A summary of what happened on the trip
- A discussion of any information learned on the trip that needs to be considered, such as customer needs or complaints
- Recommendations for any action that needs to be taken

Figure 93 Trip Report

MEMORANDUM

To: Jane Crosby, Sales Manager
From: Dirk Johnson
Date: July 11, 2012
Subject: Oklahoma sales trip

Purpose: This is an update of my sales trip last week
                    to Oklahoma City.

Summary: I called on four of our existing customers and three
                    new potential customers. The existing customers
                    (ABC, Dowd Electric, Pace Supplies, and Jumbo
                    Construction) all seemed pleased with our service.
                    The three new customers (Xecel, Jefferson Bingham,
                    and Winstead) are mainly interested in pricing.

Discussion: Jeff Brown at Xecel showed me our competitor's
                    price list. Our prices are about 10% more. Jeff
                    expressed interest in doing business with us if
                    our prices were comparable. I believe the same
                    would be true for Jefferson Bingham and Winstead.

> *Recommendation:*   I suggest we run some type of special sale or
> promotion for a specific period of time to get these
> guys to give us a try. Once they experience our
> level of service, if our prices increase later, they
> may not care.

USER GUIDE

User guides are documents about the operation of a product. The types of
user guides are:

- Large user guides, for complex products
- Software user guides, published as books, online as Web pages
  (Figure 94), or both ways
- Small user guides, written for products ranging from toasters to
  automobiles

Some user guides may include tutorials for learning to use the product.
Product tutorials are often published as separate documents (Figure 95). User
guides often include troubleshooting procedures.

User guides often include:

- Heading organization with subheadings
- Numbered and bulleted lists
- Step-by-step instructions
- Graphics and illustrations.
- Tables
- Use of boldface, italics, all caps, and different fonts to highlight
  content.
- Special notices with notes, tips, warnings, cautions, and danger
  messages

User guides also include covers (Figure 96), title pages, list of trademarks, disclaimers, warranties, license agreements, appendix items, glossaries, and an index.

The product-related content included in a user guide is usually presented in one of the following ways:

- Step-by-step instructions guide users through operating the product (Figure 97). These guides often contain:

    - Illustrations as a road map

    - Numbered lists or list bullets as formatting

- Reference information provides content about all of the components, settings, controls, and options (Figure 98). Reference information is often presented in table form.

- Getting-started information provides users with a tutorial on how to start using the product immediately (Figure 99).

- Technical specifications provide reference information for maintenance and troubleshooting.

(text continues on page 200)

Figure 94 Online User Guide

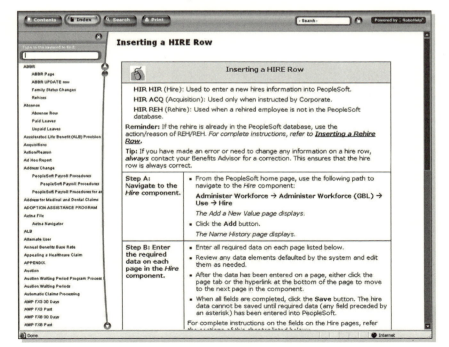

Figure 95 User Guide Tutorial

Walkthrough – Rounding

In this walkthrough, you would use the ROUND, ROUNDUP, and ROUNDDOWN functions.

Using the ROUND function

1.   Open the Round Exercise.xls file.

2.   In cell C2, enter the following formula: **=ROUNDUP(B2,0)**

3.   In cell C4, enter the formula: **=ROUND(B4,-1)**

4.   In cell C5, enter the formula: **=ROUNDDOWN(B5,0)**

	C5	f_x =ROUNDDOWN(B5,0)	
	A	**B**	**C**
1			
2	Revenues	$ 3,423,117.80	$ 3,423,118.00
3			
4	Operating Expenses	$ (1,295,371.21)	$ (1,295,370.00)
5	SG&A Expenses	$ (862,595.52)	$ (862,595.00)
6			
7	IBD	$ 1,265,151.07	
8	IBD %	36.96%	
9			
10	Average # of Dealers registered	423.62	

Note how the value in cell C2 is rounded up to the nearest whole dollar, while the value in cell C4 is rounded to the nearest whole number (because of the -1) in the formula. The value in cell C5 is also rounded down because of the ROUNDDOWN function.

5.   Save your work by clicking **File** > **Save As**, and then changing the name of the file to "**Round Exercise A**" and then click the **Save** button.

6.   Close the spreadsheet by clicking **File** > **Close**.

Figure 96 User Guide Cover

Figure 97 User Guide Instructions

PeopleSoft Basics

Changing Your Password

Changing Your Password	
Step 1: Navigate to the *Change Password* page.	▪ From the PeopleSoft home page, click the **<u>Change My Password</u>** link in the Main Menu. *The Change Password page displays* **Note**: You can also change your password from the *General Profile Information* page. **Change Password** User ID: LBCTWO Description: LBC TWO *Current Password: [ ] *New Password: [ ] *Confirm Password: [ ] [Change Password]
Step 2: Change your password.	▪ Key your current password into the **Current Password** box. ▪ Key your new password into the **New Password** box. ▪ Key your new password again into the **Confirm Password** box. ▪ Click the **Change Password** button. Your password is immediately changed in PeopleSoft and the Password Saved page displays. ### Password Saved ✔ Your password has successfully been changed. [OK] ▪ Click the **OK** button.

Password Rules to Remember:

▪ Your User ID and Password cannot be the same.
▪ Passwords must be a minimum of 7 letters and/or numbers or special characters. At least 2 of the 7 characters must be numbers.
▪ The following characters can be used in your password:
   ! @ # $ % ^ & * ( ) _ - = + \ | [ ] { } ; : / ? . < >
▪ Passwords are case sensitive. PeopleSoft-generated passwords are all upper case. You can

Figure 98 User Guide Reference Information

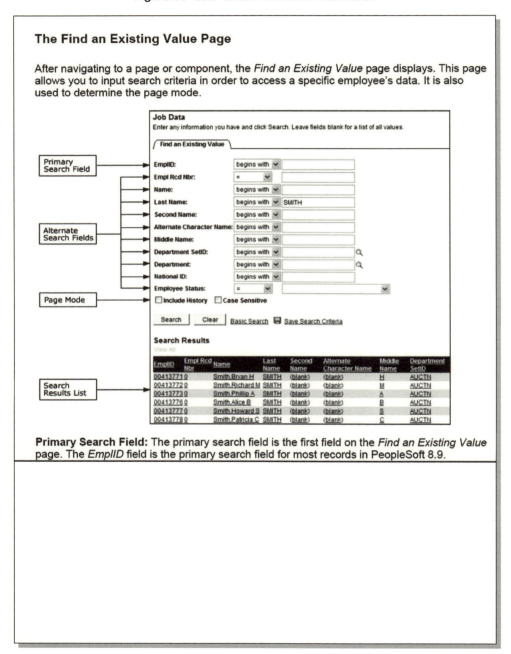

The Find an Existing Value Page

After navigating to a page or component, the *Find an Existing Value* page displays. This page allows you to input search criteria in order to access a specific employee's data. It is also used to determine the page mode.

Primary Search Field: The primary search field is the first field on the *Find an Existing Value* page. The *EmplID* field is the primary search field for most records in PeopleSoft 8.9.

Figure 99 User Guide Quick Start

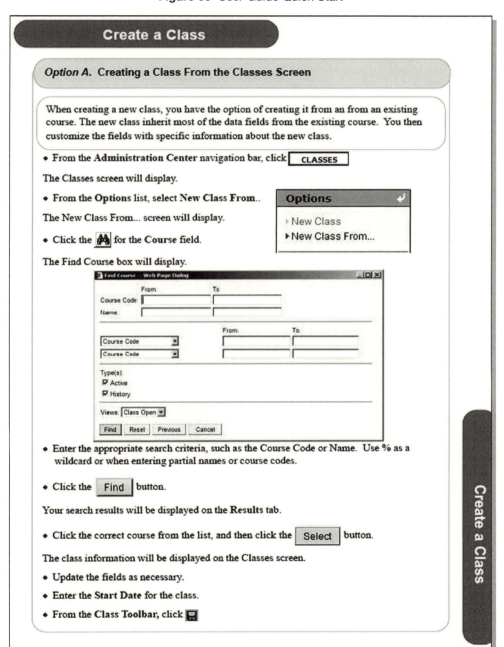

Create a Class

Option A. Creating a Class From the Classes Screen

When creating a new class, you have the option of creating it from an from an existing course. The new class inherit most of the data fields from the existing course. You then customize the fields with specific information about the new class.

- From the **Administration Center** navigation bar, click [CLASSES]

The Classes screen will display.

- From the **Options** list, select **New Class From..**

The New Class From... screen will display.

- Click the 🔍 for the **Course** field.

Options
▸ New Class
▸ New Class From...

The Find Course box will display.

- Enter the appropriate search criteria, such as the Course Code or Name. Use % as a wildcard or when entering partial names or course codes.

- Click the [Find] button.

Your search results will be displayed on the **Results** tab.

- Click the correct course from the list, and then click the [Select] button.

The class information will be displayed on the Classes screen.

- Update the fields as necessary.
- Enter the **Start Date** for the class.
- From the **Class Toolbar**, click 💾

Create a Class

WARNING LETTER

Warning or **discipline letters** are written to make an employee aware of a problem and to define potential disciplinary action. A warning letter becomes part of an employee's personnel file and may be used later during the termination process.

When writing a warning letter, consider these tips (Figure 100):

- Start the letter by stating briefly what events led to the written warning. Include specific situations, dates, and times.

- Identify your expectations for the employee and what behavior the employee needs to change.

- Warn the employee that disciplinary action may have to be taken if the behavior is not corrected.

    - Provide details about what the disciplinary action may include.

    - State that failure to correct the situation may result in termination.

Warning letters are typically written to:

- Document a reprimand.

- Warn an employee for breach of policy.

- Warn an employee for poor performance.

- Reprimand an employee for poor attendance or lateness.

- Warn tenants in a rental property.

- Warn customers about a credit suspension.

Figure 100 Warning Letter

Credit Corp America
4300 Interstate Parkway
Dallas, TX 75301
June 2, 2012

Mary Sullivan
6426 Lakewood Blvd
Dallas, TX 75214

Dear Mrs. Sullivan:

As you will recall, the sales quota for our customer representatives
is $10,000 per month. I discussed with you at the end of April that it
was important for you to achieve this quota each and every month.
For the month of May, your sales totaled only $5,500.

Company policy states that any customer representative who fails to
achieve his/her sales quota for two consecutive months is subject to
termination. As a result of this situation, this letter will serve as a warning,
and a copy will be placed in your personnel file. To avoid termination,
you will need to achieve your quota for the month of June.

If you know of any problems that will prevent you from reaching these
goals, or if you wish to discuss this matter with me in more detail,
please arrange for a meeting.

Yours,

Mary Ann Lemer

Mary Ann Lemer
Vice President of Sales

WEB SITES

Writing for a **Web site** is different from writing for print.

■ Writing for print is linear in nature, whereas writing for the Web is nonlinear.

■ Web page content is usually chunked and packaged, so that a reader can quickly scan the page and decide whether to read more. (Readers spend very little time reading text on an individual Web page.)

■ Web pages feature highlighted keywords, extensive use of subheadings, bulleted lists, and normally half the word length of a similar paper document.

When writing content for a Web site, consider these tips (Figure 101):

■ Tone down promotional marketing hype and focus instead on reference and helpful information.

■ Use an objective rather than a subjective tone.

■ Use the active voice for Web content.

■ Show numbers as numerals in all Web content.

　■ Numerals are easier to scan and take up less room.

■ Spell out large numbers, such as a million, billion, and trillion, because the words are shorter than the numerals.

When writing headlines for Web articles:

■ Keep headlines short and format them in bold.

■ Summarize the article so that users will know enough to determine whether they want to read it.

■ Include the most important keywords first in the headline because readers often scan only the first few words of a headline.

　■ Use keywords that match common user search criteria in search engines.

■ Substitute commonly known words for technical jargon.

■ Use generic names rather than brand names.

- Make the average headline five words.

When writing a Web article, consider the following:

- Use the inverted pyramid approach that is often used by journalists where you begin the article by telling the reader the conclusion, followed by important supporting information, and then end by providing background details.
- Use down-to-earth informal language to make the content easy to understand.
- Include hyperlinks to reference sources for added credibility.
- Use humor with caution because of the wide variety of user preferences.
- Use approximately 60% fewer words than you would if you were writing the same content for print.
- Chunk the content into sections and move nice-to-know content to other pages, and include hyperlinks to this content in the main article.
- Illustrations should always have a caption and complement the text rather than used just to make the page flashy.
- Segment the text to make it easier to scan the document.
  - Break up long paragraphs into smaller segments.
  - Include a heading that describes the subject of each segment, and capitalize the first letter of each word.
  - Include subheadings where appropriate, and capitalize only the first word.
- For lists of any kind, use bullet lists.
- Use the three aspects of rhetoric: ethos, pathos, and logos.
  - Ethos—Establish the credibility of the author by including references and hyperlinks to your sources.
  - Pathos—Make an appeal to the reader's emotions by writing from the reader's point of view.
  - Logos—Appeal to the reader's logic by providing statistical facts and convincing examples

Figure 101 Web Site

WHITE PAPERS

White papers are written to introduce an innovative product or technology to the industry, emphasize the unique qualities and advantages of a product or service, help influence customer buying decisions, and are the beginning steps in the creation of a product marketing strategy.

When preparing to write a white paper, read other white papers available on the Internet and look for successful models. Consider how the white paper will be published: paper-based or on a Web site.

When writing a white paper (Figure 102):

- Define the audience and understand their concerns.

- Be aware of the time investment required by the audience to read your white paper.
    - Make sure it is engaging and captures the audience's attention.

- Start with a one-paragraph executive summary with the key points the audience needs to know.

- State the problem faced by the customer that the product or service can solve.

- Describe the product and include the following details:
    - How the product was designed
    - What industry standards were used or considered
    - What type of testing was conducted on the product or service
    - What best practices were learned

- Keep a positive tone.

- Use the active voice.

- Avoid jargon and keep the presentation as nontechnical as possible.

- Include diagrams and illustrations.

- Explain how the product resolves the problem stated earlier.

- Tie the product to the problem, and include case study evidence of how the product solved the problem.

- Include testimonials and interview quotes, if available.

- Conclude by summarizing the benefits and discussing the return on investment for customers.

- Mention future product development and timelines for release.

Figure 102 White Paper

PUTTING CITIZENS FIRST:
Transforming Online Governement

A White Paper Written for the Presidential Transition Team by

The Federal Web Managers Council

Current and former members of the Federal Web Managers Council who contributed to this paper: Bev Godwin, General Services Administration/USA.gov (Executive Sponsor); Sheila Campbell, General Services Administration/USA.gov (co-chair); Rachel Flagg, Dept. of Housing and Urban Development (co-chair); Melissa Allen, Dept. of Interior; Andy Bailey, Dept. of Labor; Les Benito, Dept. of Defense; Joyce Bounds, Dept. of Veterans Affairs; Nicole Burton, General Services Administration/USA.gov; Bruce Carter, Social Security Administration (retired); Natalie Davidson, General Services Administration/USA.gov; Kate Donohue, Dept. of Treasury; Brian Dunbar, NASA; Tim Evans, Social Security Administration; Kellie Feeney, Dept. of Transportation; Sam Gallagher, Dept. of Housing and Urban Development; Colleen Hope, Dept. of State; Ron Jones, Dept. of Commerce/NOAA; Tina Kelley; Dept. of Justice; Gwynne Kostin, Dept. of Homeland Security; Jeffrey Levy, EPA; Beth Martin, Dept. of Health and Human Services; Leilani Martinez, GSA/GobiernoUSA.gov; Suzanne Nawrot, Dept. of Energy; Russell O'Neill, General Services Administration/USA.gov; Tom Parisi, Dept. of Treasury/IRS; Vic Powell, USDA; Rezaur Rahman, Advisory Council on Historic Preservation; Eric Ramoth, Dept. of Housing and Urban Development; Rand Ruggieri, Dept. of Commerce; Richard Stapleton, Dept. of Health and Human Services; Kim Taylor, USDA; Kirk Winters, Dept. of Education

We welcome your questions and comments. Please contact the Federal Web Managers Council co-chairs, Sheila Campbell (Sheila.campbell@gsa.gov) and Rachel Flagg (Rachel.flagg@hud.gov).

Introduction

This White Paper recommends specific strategies for revolutionizing how the U.S. Government delivers online services to the American people. It was developed by the Federal Web Managers Council, comprised of Cabinet agency Web Directors.

The current state of government online communications

The importance of the Internet has grown exponentially over the last decade, but the government's ability to provide online services to the American people hasn't grown at the same pace. Building this capacity will present one of the biggest challenges—and most promising opportunities—for President-elect Obama. We need to build on the groundswell of citizen participation in the presidential campaign and make people's everyday interactions with their government easier and more transparent.

It won't be an easy task. There are approximately 24,000 U.S. Government websites now online (but no one knows the exact number). Many websites tout organizational achievements instead of effectively delivering basic information and services. Many web managers don't have access to social media tools because of legal, security, privacy, and internal policy concerns. Many agencies focus more on technology and website infrastructure than improving content and service delivery. Technology should not drive our business decisions, but rather help us serve the needs of the American people. Here's the result when communication takes a backseat to technology:

> "Often I can find the page on a government site that's supposed to contain the information I need, but I can't make heads or tails of it. I recently tried to Google a specific requirement for dependent care flex accounts. Although I got to the correct page, it didn't answer my question. The links took me to the typical, poorly written tax guidance. Where did I get the answer to my question? On Wikipedia."

We're working to address these problems. We've built a network of over 1,500 federal, state, and local web professionals across the country to share best practices; we created a large-scale training program for web managers; and we're working to support the use of social media while also addressing important privacy, security, and legal implications.

While our efforts have been very successful, a high-level mandate from the new Administration is needed to quickly and radically transform government websites.

A bold, new vision for the future

President-elect Obama should be able to promise the American people that when they need government information and services online, they will be able to:

Figure 102 *(continued)*

- Easily find relevant, accurate, and up-to-date information;
- Understand information the first time they read it;
- Complete common tasks efficiently;
- Get the same answer whether they use the web, phone, email, live chat, read a brochure, or visit in-person;
- Provide feedback and ideas and hear what the government will do with them;
- Access critical information if they have a disability or aren't proficient in English.

The recommendations below are designed to help the new Administration increase the efficiency, transparency, accountability, and participation between government and the American people. Some of these changes can be implemented quickly and at minimal cost. Others will require significant changes in how agencies conduct business and may require shifts in how they fund web communications.

Establish Web Communications as a core government business function
One of the biggest problems we face in improving government websites is that many agencies still view their website as an IT project rather than as a core business function. Many government websites lack a dedicated budget. Only a minority of agencies have developed strong web policies and management controls. Some have hundreds of "legacy" websites with outdated or irrelevant content. With limited resources, many find it difficult to solicit regular customer input and take quick action to improve their sites. While there are many effective government websites, most web teams are struggling to manage the amount of online content the government produces every day.

- Agencies should be required to fund their "virtual" office space as part of their critical infrastructure, in the same way they fund their "bricks and mortar" office space.
- Agencies should be required to appoint an editor-in-chief for every website they maintain, as do the top commercial websites. This person should be given appropriate funding and authority to develop and enforce web policies and publishing standards, including ensuring that prime real estate on government websites is dedicated to helping people find the information they need.
- OPM should develop standard job descriptions and core training requirements so agencies can hire and retain highly qualified experts in web content and new media—not just IT specialists.

Help the public complete common government tasks efficiently

The U.S. economy loses millions of hours of "citizen productivity" every year when people can't efficiently accomplish basic government tasks online, such as filling out a form, applying for a loan, or checking eligibility for a government program. This adds to people's dissatisfaction with their government.

■ Agencies should be required and funded to identify their core online customer tasks, and to develop service standards and performance benchmarks for completing those tasks. If the core customer tasks are not yet online, agencies should determine whether or not those tasks can be made available online, and if so, develop a plan for making them available online within one year.

■ The Government should use social media, not just to create transparency, but also to help people accomplish their core tasks. For example, agencies could post instructional videos on YouTube to explain how to apply for a small business loan or learn about Medicare benefits. To do this, the government must ensure that federal employees who need access to social media tools have them, and that these new ways of delivering content are available to all, including people with disabilities.

■ The new Administration should develop government-wide guidelines for disseminating content in universally accessible formats (data formats, news feeds, mobile, video, podcasts, etc.), and on non-government sites such as YouTube, Wikipedia, and SecondLife. To remain relevant, government needs to take our content to where people already are on the Web, rather than just expecting people will come to government websites. Having guidelines will ensure that we're part of the larger "online information ecosystem," without compromising the integrity of government information.

Clean up the clutter so people can find what they need online

President-elect Obama will inherit thousands of U.S. government websites. We have too much content to categorize, search, and manage effectively, and there is no comprehensive system for removing or archiving old or underused content. Some agencies have posted competing websites on similar topics, creating duplication of effort and causing confusion for the public. Much government web content is written in "governmentese" instead of plain language.

■ The Government should set stricter standards for approving new, or renewing existing, government websites. All federally owned, managed, and/or directly funded websites must be hosted on .gov, .mil or fed.us domains. Where agency missions are related, a lead agency should be appointed to coordinate the online

Figure 102 *(continued)*

"information lane," and all other agencies should defer to the lead agency for posting comprehensive government information on that topic. This will reduce duplication, save money, and help consumers find accurate information.

- Agencies should be required and funded to conduct regular content reviews, to ensure their online content is accurate, relevant, mission-related, and written in plain language. They should have a process for archiving content that is no longer in frequent use and no longer required on the website.

- Agencies should be funded and required to follow the latest best practices in web search. This will improve the quality and findability of online government information, and help agencies deliver the services most requested by their customers.

Engage the public in a dialogue to improve our customer service

Agencies often don't have resources to effectively manage customer input. For those that do, they must go through a clearance process before they can survey the public (requirements of the Paperwork Reduction Act, which was enacted before many agencies even had websites). Many web pages are developed without regular feedback or testing with customers. When people do provide feedback or ideas, they often never hear what the government will do with their suggestions.

- Agencies should be required and funded to regularly solicit public opinion and analyze customers' online preferences—just as Amazon, eBay, and other top commercial websites do. This can be done on an "opt-in" basis and without tracking personally identifiable information by using blogs, online surveys, a "Citizens Insight Panel" (such as that used by the Canadian government), or similar tools. Agencies should be required and funded to do user testing before undertaking major improvements to any current website, or launching a new website.

- Agencies should use their website to publish a summary of common customer comments and explain the actions they are taking in response to the feedback. Doing so will create better transparency and accountability.

Ensure the public gets the same answer whether they use the web, phone, email, print, or visit in-person

Agencies communicate with citizens via many different "delivery channels," including web, email, publications, live chats, blogs, podcasts, videos, wikis, virtual online worlds, and more. But it's difficult to ensure timeliness and consistency when various delivery channels are managed by different divisions within an agency.

- Agencies should provide multiple ways for people to contact them and ensure that information is consistent across all channels. They should be funded to coordinate all types of content targeted to the general public (web, publications, call center, email, common questions, web chat, etc.). Agencies should be rewarded for delivering consistent information, both within agencies and across government.

Ensure underserved populations can access critical information online

Agencies are required to provide online information that's readily accessible by people with disabilities, as well as to people with limited English proficiency. However, few agencies have the funding, training or resources to meet these obligations.

- The government should establish standards and guidelines for multilingual websites, and agencies should be funded and staffed with qualified bilingual web content professionals who can create and maintain them. This will help newcomers learn about the rights and responsibilities of living in the U.S.
- Agencies should receive adequate resources to make their websites fully accessible to people with disabilities and meet requirements of the Rehabilitation Act. The new Administration should invest in government-wide solutions, such as captioning software to make videos and webcasts accessible to people with disabilities.

Conclusion

By harnessing the collaborative nature of the web, the new Administration has the potential to engage the public like never before. The web can foster better communication and allow people to participate in improving the operations of their government. By listening to our customers we can provide better services, focus on their most pressing needs, and spend their tax dollars efficiently. We're confident that President-elect Obama will appoint leaders who will invest in the web as a strategic asset and make these goals a reality. The millions of Americans who interact with their government online expect and deserve no less.